TONE

from the Committee to Investigate Atmosphere

TONE

SOFIA SAMATAR

KATE ZAMBRENO

Columbia University Press
New York

Columbia University Press
Publishers Since 1893
New York   Chichester, West Sussex
cup.columbia.edu
Copyright © 2024 Sofia Samatar and Kate Zambreno

Library of Congress Cataloging-in-Publication Data

Names: Samatar, Sofia, author. | Zambreno, Kate, author.
Title: Tone / Sofia Samatar and Kate Zambreno.
Description: New York : Columbia University Press, 2023. |
Includes bibliographical references.
Identifiers: LCCN 2023024116 (print) | LCCN 2023024117 (ebook) |
ISBN 9780231211208 (hardback) | ISBN 9780231211215
(trade paperback) | ISBN 9780231558792 (ebook)
Subjects: LCSH: Affect (Psychology) in literature. | Authors and
readers. | Discourse analysis, Literary. | LCGFT: Literary criticism.
Classification: LCC PN56.A43 S26 2023 (print) | LCC PN56.A43
(ebook) | DDC 801/.9—dc23/eng/20230728
LC record available at https://lccn.loc.gov/2023024116
LC ebook record available at https://lccn.loc.gov/2023024117

Printed and bound by CPI Group (UK) Ltd, Croydon, CR0 4YY

Cover design: Julia Kushnirsky
Cover image: Portia Munson, *Blue Vanity*, 2022 (detail)
Courtesy of Portia Munson and P·P·O·W, New York

CONTENTS

TONE

TONE

I

FRONT MATTER, OR THE ZONE OF OUR MUTUAL SENSITIVITY

Abstract

We began with a sound. At first it was faint; then it slowly increased until it became distracting, almost unbearable. We began with a barely perceptible odor, which, as it intensified, prompted us to investigate its source. We began with a light, with the ambience that is literature. Where did it come from? Was it in the room with us, did it emanate from our body? We began with this body, which was a collective reading body, the zone of our mutual sensitivity, our ground.

Keywords

Affect, ecology, collectivity, vibration, architecture
Fog, dust, rot, snow, light
Distance, echo, pressure, gesture, blur

Significance Statement

We are still unsure, at the present time, whether we can make the statement for any significance. Assuming that we follow after this feeling or mutual sensitivity, we hope that there will be meaning derived from our samplings. Furthermore: We hope to listen. We have formulated a problem. What is tone? We will attempt to explore this through observations, stimulations, and methods.

Introduction

It began as a desire for the collective. For the us that is us and beyond us. We desired to be together in the same space, were intrigued by this collaborative experiment, the friction of rubbing against each other, the irritation of collaboration, as Fred Moten and Stefano Harney, together, have said. The longing was to reach beyond the limitation of the first-person, to find something like a commons. How tired we were of the us that was us, how much we wanted to transcend this Name Name and that Name Name and all of what it meant, our names, our skin. To formalize the shedding we were already experiencing, in our epistolary relationship, in the other ways we have formed community, in the literature of quavering subjectivities in relation to others. Someone else has entered the chat. And so here we are.

Was this tone? What was tone? Was it everywhere, in the atmosphere? Reading the collective animal of the novels we loved, that we wanted to read and reread together. What was it we were hearing? What was it we were feeling? Could we diffuse all this into a theory or theories of the tonal? Throughout this could we write as one, or as multiple, into a consistent tonality?

The study of tone, it seemed to us, was a project that could not be undertaken alone. What creates the vibe of a room? The other people inside it: the combined resonance of their voices, shrill or caressing, lengthening and tightening with the shifts in their massed and consolidated feelings, the warmth that emanates from their clothes, their hair, the odor of nervousness, of joy or resentment, of an incipient crush. And if the room is empty, there is a trace in the air of those who have recently left. How far is it possible to analyze a fading perfume? Or the furniture, creased and marked by pressure and sweat. The impulse behind the choice of the light fixture. The hands that have crafted, transported, and polished these things. In the floorboards, stains of blood and tears from long before our arrival, soot from when there was a stove here, hairs from so many cats and dogs. A trapped bee thumps at the windowpane. We were drawn to the subject of tone because its vibrations informed us that we belonged to it; it did not belong to us.

To enter that space of belonging was delight. It was where proper names became absurd, where private expertise rubbed off in the mix of forces. There writing, the loneliest practice, was revealed as hubbub and embrace. Language emerged from abstraction and became contour. We agreed to meet there. But where, exactly? *There.* That was tone. We were fascinated by the difficulty of describing this space, this atmosphere. It charmed us that so many before us had failed to define it, thrown up their hands, and given up, content simply to agree that it exists. "The strange thing about life," wrote Virginia Woolf, "is that though the nature of it must have been apparent to every one for hundreds of years, no one has left any adequate account of it."

A textual rendezvous. We agreed to meet in two objects made of paper, opened and read in the same general period of time: sometimes at the same instant, sometimes in overlapping hours, and sometimes in a relay, as if one hand had passed the book to the other. At times we were reading both paper and electronic books. We were reading in more than one language. We were scrutinizing two chapters at once. And we found ourselves together on the same train, the same beach, the same street corner, in a shared light, taking in the scent of that place, its color. We became chimerical, a creature of fiction with keyboard fingertips. Our lair was a document in the cloud. Our habitat was literature. With tentative, curious, childlike movements, we tapped the ground, exploring the timbre of writing, its grain.

When did our correspondence on tone begin? It began within the beginning of fall and the intensity of the semester, overworked, burnt out, yet still gleaming with literature. It's always nice to have something on the side. It was a gift to ourselves, a form of care, thinking with each other. To go back in. To think about thinking about tone. Which was also thinking about love and friendship and community. Collaboration seemed fun or hopeful. It made sense for us now.

And yet we find our findings resistant to being introduced. This introduction must therefore be abbreviated. However, we still want to introduce ourselves, as much as that is possible. We are the Committee to Investigate Atmosphere. Thus begins the body of the text, our body.

II

FOG, OR A GRADUAL ACCUMULATION

AT THE beginning of our investigation, we asked our students to examine the tone of Nella Larsen's *Quicksand*. Our students described the tone of this novel as "gray." They cited the following paragraph:

> Well into Helga's second year in Denmark, came an indefinite discontent. Not clear, but vague, like a storm gathering far on the horizon. It was long before she would admit that she was less happy than she had been during her first year in Copenhagen, but she knew that it was so. And this subconscious knowledge added to her growing restlessness and little mental insecurity. She desired ardently to combat this wearing down of her satisfaction with her life, with herself. But she didn't know how.

Our students described the tone of this novel as "a gradual accumulation." They said it was ominous. They called it "fog."

But where does tone reside, and what are its signs? Clouds are gray, a storm is gray, and so, for our students, this passage from *Quicksand* exemplifies grayness. But we felt that tone could not reside in the image of a storm. Is it not, rather, the fact that the passage contains no images at all, nothing that indicates life but a storm that is only a metaphor—is it not this absence that makes the passage gray? Instead of word pictures, we encounter words that describe a blankness: *indefinite, not clear, vague, subconscious, little, wearing down.* Beneath this layer of words that express nothing certain, Helga's "ardent desire" for "combat" gutters out like a candle in the smog.

If not in the storm, we investigate where to locate tone in *Quicksand*. In Helga Crane, in the narrator, are they one and the same? Is it somehow in the ether? Is ether like a fog? A line from Etel Adnan appears in our collective bubble, then disappears, because we are thinking of Etel Adnan: "Fog has covered everything in gray absolute." Is the tone in the novel like the "soft gloom" of the opening sentence, the ambience where Helga Crane sits alone in her chosen solitude, attempting to find herself again after her long day of giving herself without anything being given back? From our own couches, exhausted, *a wearing down of life*, we continue to reside within Helga Crane's room that opens *Quicksand*. The gloom is soft, and hers, like the silk robes she wraps herself in. It is in the cocoon of Helga Crane's room that we might locate something like mood or atmosphere, sinking into the soft fabrics and silky sulkiness, the "framing of light and shade." Even on the first two pages, we are in this room, which is her tone—but whose is it? A tone is perhaps a room that we inhabit and are inhabited by. It is the interior that surrounds and the exterior that invades. Something we must listen to, be attuned to, within the necessity of silence. Are these paragraphs, here, the rooms in which we attempt to meet? We take some time to think about this. We settle into our fogs, attempting to think, to find space, amid so many other pressures. We take residence within tone, wherever it may be. Is it here? Where we are now? Our investigations cloud, become vague, with occasional clarity. Can we proceed like this, a gradual accumulation?

We wonder if it's a coincidence that we commence the first meetings of the Committee to Investigate Atmosphere here, in these paragraphs, within a setting of higher education. *Quicksand* begins with Helga Crane deciding to quit her job at a Southern teachers college. She is warned that if she does so she'll never be hired again in the South. She doesn't care. She sits in her room and stews in her resentment and discontent. Nella Larsen is philosophizing here about the obvious nonrecognition between teacher and student, about all of the language of community, when instead higher education in the novel is an alienating machine, the arrogance and condescension on the part of the faculty and the simmering disdain on the part of the students, much as Mark Fisher conceptualizes in *Capitalist Realism*. Can capitalist realism be an atmosphere, an "organizing quality of feeling"? Reporting from the airless rooms where we are currently being asked to hold our classes, our faces obscured, we think of Helga Crane briefly escaping the claustrophobic rigidity of her environment by walking through campus, communing with the trees, a moment of breath within the text. We think of Fred Moten and Saidiya Hartman in conversation about the "Black outdoors": Hartman speaking of the energy of producing the thought of the outside while inside. The attempt to create, says Hartman, an opening.

Can we create an opening here? We wish to investigate this pervasive *irritation* that Sianne Ngai writes of as the ugly feeling of *Quicksand*. At first we are told that Helga Crane's irritation comes as an intrusion of thoughts (the intrusion of the outside, inside). We are interested in the way Ngai frames irritation as a time release, an ongoing mood over a period of time. But there is within this reading the assumption that readers are irritated by Helga Crane as well, that irritation is the main affect of such a character, whom Ngai sees as a descendant of Melville's Bartleby, that there is a fundamental ambivalence to how Helga Crane is characterized. The narrator of *Quicksand* describes a "faint hint of offishness" hovering about Helga, "an arrogance that stirred in people a peculiar irritation." This distant manner, which protected her as a sensitive, miserable child, has never left her. She is unconscious of it. All unaware, she carries this bad air about with her, this vaguely repellent aura that, Ngai writes, affects even readers of *Quicksand*. Ngai moves from positing that Helga's lack of responsiveness to a racist incident "is likely to irritate the reader" to analyzing "our irritation" with Helga, a reaction that is no longer merely likely but inevitable. For this novel blocks us, Ngai contends. It refuses our sympathy.

Reading *Ugly Feelings*, we loved the barbed subversiveness Ngai ascribes to irritation, and we were taken with the idea that *Quicksand* champions the right to opacity for Black artists, the "right to *not* express." We are drawn to the idea of passivity as a form of resistance—one whose distance and ambivalence cause irritation. The only problem is, we've never been irritated with Helga. Never, never. She is putting on her brown oxfords and blue twill suit. In the rainy, leaden day, she is going to the employment office. We understand her precarity, the constant buzzing of crisis. She is going to Copenhagen. She is letting some Danes cut up her green velvet dress. In the slashed, skimpy dress, with beads and long earrings, she poses on a red satin couch. We have never been mystified by her increasingly desperate shifts from room to room. Her sudden decisions to quit, to be a quitter, to refuse. Those terrible people in Copenhagen! The smug James Vayle, whom she almost married, and the sanctimonious Reverend Mr. Pleasant Green she did marry in the end! No, we have never been blocked, never shut out, never found her repressed or inexpressive, as she "passionately, tearfully, incoherently" speaks of her childhood, as she weeps "with great racking sobs" and finally yells "like one insane, drowning every other clamor, while torrents of tears streamed down her face."

Isn't Helga Crane's violently flinging her work materials into the wastebasket a form of praxis? Why should we be lovable when institutions don't love us? Yet we are told Helga Crane rubs some people the wrong way—like a chafing—and Sianne Ngai reads irritation as an affect worn close to the body, Helga Crane's body, covered in an armor of satin, velvet, and pride, which others see as hauteur or aloofness. We wonder if this has something to do with class. Why, Helga Crane, do you have such stylish clothes, the good Christian people wonder at church, in the passage we have just cited. And for her "bare arms and neck growing out of the clinging red dress," they immediately call her a scarlet woman, a jezebel. And yet we know how horribly lonely and lost she feels, alone in that big city, desperately poor, nearing bottom. Always on the verge of weeping, so she shuts down, shuts in tremendous feeling. That moment of observing Helga Crane's unconscious offishness, perhaps it is by a "covert omniscient narrator," as Ngai observes, but perhaps Larsen is worming, wonderfully, into a close interior point of view, an acknowledgment of not having awareness of what puts everyone off Helga Crane; this is something of tone, this narrative gaze porous and at tension between deep feeling and consciousness and physical exterior, or one's perception of how others perceive one's physical exterior, that also manages something in its syntax like mimicry of judgmental, even horrible voices. Perhaps the offishness is more an off-gas, a diffusion; perhaps we are getting closer to locating the tone in Larsen's novel. We suspect it is what we call a radical opacity, what Ngai calls "psychological illegibility," that the church people, the employment office, yes, perhaps *some* readers, find irritating or ambivalent. But that is because they are moralizing Helga Crane, wanting her to be just a little more forthcoming, a little more transparent, more grateful, more sympathetic, more (tonally) warm, less cold, when looking for work, when alienated from this exhausting and extractive labor. If she puts others off by her tone, they will close the book on her. Aren't you, these readers wonder, these readers of Helga Crane's face and body, by that we also mean her tone, being a little proud? It is difficult for these readers of Helga Crane to translate her passivity; perhaps there is something repulsive about it. Are we reading something in your tone?

As we considered the atmosphere of *Quicksand* as tonally gray, we reflected that black + white = gray. But also, in the racial iconography of our country, black + white = yellow, the color of the mixed-race Helga with her "skin like yellow satin." Yellow is a warm tone, while gray is cool. In the course of our investigation, we encountered a story by Arthur Conan Doyle called "The Adventure of the Yellow Face." In this story, a Mr. Grant Munro seeks the aid of the great detective Sherlock Holmes to solve a mystery involving Grant Munro's wife. The wife—a widow before her marriage—has been sneaking out of the house to a nearby cottage, a place that appears deserted, except that at times a horrible face appears in one of the windows, a face with "something unnatural and inhuman" about it. Mr. Grant Munro cannot ascribe a gender to this face. He describes it as "a livid chalky white," then as a "yellow livid face." It is eerily devoid of expression, "with something set and rigid about it which was shockingly unnatural." It is in fact a mask, as Holmes discovers. When he enters the house and peels it away, a Black child is revealed, "coal black," "with all her white teeth flashing"—Mrs. Grant Munro's daughter by her deceased Black husband. The woman has been concealing the child out of shame. But once the child's blackness has been revealed, all is well. The specter of passing raised by the weird, inscrutable white/yellow face disperses—the child, Mrs. Grant Munro assures us, "is darker far than ever her father was." Show us how you really feel and who you really are. Dr. Watson, who narrates this story, bursts out laughing "out of sympathy" with the child's merriment, this child who laughs but never speaks, the "little creature" who, when Mrs. Grant Munro calls her "her mother's pet," runs to nestle against the lady. As for Mr. Grant Munro, he picks up the child and kisses her in a gesture, Watson recalls, "of which I love to think." So warm, the yellow light falling from the window, the golden track of lamplight, the magnanimous heart of the good Mr. Grant Munro! Reading "The Adventure of the Yellow Face," we thought of the claustrophobic atmosphere of Charlotte Perkins Gilman's "The Yellow Wallpaper," another tale in which masculine control takes the form of warmth—"'Bless her little heart!' said he with a big hug, 'she shall be as sick as she pleases!'"—a tale of isolation, imprisonment for one's own good, the diagnosing eye of the doctor/detective, and a yellow glow, taking the form of a "sickly sulphur tint," that covers a woman's faint form like a mask. Tone, we saw, might also be about interior decor. "The Adventure of the Yellow Face" pursues the interior, helping itself to a liberal handful of feeling from the genre Sianne Ngai describes as "sentimental 'mulatta' fiction," a genre from which, she writes, Nella Larsen deliberately distanced herself with her gaunt gray novels, resolutely cool.

But there is something mournful in this coolness, something that touches us, that gives us a pang. We remember Helga's longing for bright colors, how she hates wearing black, brown, and gray, how she dwells with delight on the memory of a Black girl in a flaming orange dress. "Why, she wondered, didn't someone write *A Plea for Color*?" But she can't write it. Instead she goes about in a grayish mask, this set, rigid face that puts people off—better that, she thinks, than the exaggerations, the flashing white teeth, the minstrel antics that horrify her in Copenhagen, where she watches two Black men clown onstage, a sight the Danish Axel Olsen, whose marriage proposal she will reject, drinks in avidly. Better the blankness of her closed eyes as she lies in bed exhausted, worn out with childbearing, than the preaching of her husband, the Reverend Mr. Pleasant Green, described as a "yellow" and "unctuous" man, a warm-toned character, soothing, bidding her to trust in the Lord and accept her fate. A mask, this novel suggests, is preferable to a gape or grimace. We thought again of the child in "The Adventure of the Yellow Face," whose mask reveals a grin presented as a real expression but which Helga knows, and we know, and Paul Laurence Dunbar knew, is only another mask. With a sudden, dizzy feeling, we thought: It's masks all the way down. We felt again the soft gloom. The paper crane, folded over and over. We remembered our student who wrote, describing the difficulty of determining tone in *Quicksand*, "If I were forced to say a tone exists, I would call it Helga."

So let us reside within this speculation in order to investigate: Could Helga actually be tone? Perhaps Helga *is* tone. What would that mean? *If we were forced to say a tone exists.* Tone is, according to Sianne Ngai, a form of feeling, giving tone more dimensionality than the New Critics, I. A. Richards and the rest, who saw tone merely as relation. The affective stance toward the world (of the reader? the other characters?). Perhaps we can think of tone as something like a collective mood. Is tone the way Helga Crane thinks through her feelings? The space of her consciousness? How she views others, both human and nonhuman? Perhaps the book Nella Larsen writes, the tone Helga Crane sets, is actually *A Plea for Color.* Let us go back to that opening room, the room of furnishings and clothes where the teacher has spent the majority of her income to surround herself with beauty. The shiny brass bowl holding sunbursts of flowers. The blue patterned carpet. And her. Dressed in her green and gold nightgown and brocaded mules. The skin like yellow satin. The "pale amber loveliness" of her face. Feet the color of biscuits. Throughout there is a painterly eye toward the many shades of Black skin, the "luminous tones lurking in their dusky skins." The tone when describing this complex figuration of blackness in the world of the novel is one of melancholy, suffused with beauty and grief. The detail and care with which Nella Larsen, through Helga Crane, describes the visual world, describes tone—that is the collective mood, that is relation. Helga Crane's love of extravagant clothes—her desire to find joy in colors—is what keeps her apart from the dull office workers in their browns and navy blues, from those at her institution who have lectured her on the vulgarity of gaudy palettes. Yes, love of dark purples, royal blues, rich greens, deep reds. And if tone resides within rooms in a novel, tonality is shown looking out the window—how Helga Crane views landscape in glimpses—the sunlight dissolves from thick orange to pale yellow, the wisps of clouds seen through the window of the segregated train en route to the cruel indifference of the big city. We are still stuck—sorry—on the assertion that readers of *Quicksand* are irritated by the nondefinite sources of suffering in the novel. Aren't suffering and oppression so often diffuse, which is why they can so often be dismissed as unreal? We can just turn to the scene on the segregated train, Helga Crane observing the skin tones of her fellow riders, feeling apartness at their sense of togetherness and family. The physical pain at the smell of stale food and smoke, the claustrophobia, the crush (Ngai observes that her apartness here is class-inflected). The white man who walks through and spits—spits!—in the communal drinking water. How was anyone to respond? They must be passive to this ambient racism; there was no possible response except for Helga Crane to look out the window. This is something like tone in this novel. Looking at the crowded car, looking out the window (let us remind ourselves to return to windows).

If we were forced to say a tone exists in Nella Larsen's *Quicksand*, we amend, we would not call it Helga. We would call it *Helga Crane*. The name, repeated so often throughout the novel, establishes and maintains a distance between the narrator and Helga. One does not think of oneself in this formal way, as *Helga Crane*, as if introduced a moment ago at a party. Nor does one meditate, alone in one's room, on one's own pale amber face or biscuit-colored feet. It is in fact "an observer" who "would have thought" the young woman well suited to her room, whose attention "would fasten" on her eyes, brows, and mouth. Alone, she is not alone. The observer is there. We were reading Dionne Brand, who wrote: "One enters a room and history follows; one enters a room and history precedes. History is already seated in the chair in the empty room when one arrives." We thought: *There are no empty rooms*. Helga Crane, migratory bird, are you seeking an empty room in Chicago, in New York, in Copenhagen, in a small Alabama town? A blocked migration. Wings beating against the door of no return. Forever off course in the wind, in the storm, in what Christina Sharpe calls *the weather*. Sharpe writes of slavery as "atmospheric density," of antiblackness as climate. We thought of Nella Larsen writing into this ongoing weather. We began to consider tone not only as sound but also as skin tone, which covers a surface and renders it opaque.

Everywhere now there are masks, and who is allowed to have a face? What privilege to be allowed to say how one really feels? We speak from the slight shudder of current protocols. Is there a chill here? We are always outside. Can you hear us through our masks, should we speak up? Our summoning of *empty rooms* in *Quicksand* makes us think of *empty wardrobes*. We reach for the recent translation by Margaret Jull Costa of Maria Judite De Carvalho's novel of that name, remarkable as well for its tone of pique. Of our heroine, the widow Dora Rosário, who manages an antiques store, we are told in the opening page that she seldom spoke, her face a mask: "She would sit quite still then, her face a blank, like someone poised on the edge of an ellipsis or standing hesitantly at the sea's edge in winter, and at such moments, all the light would go out of her eyes as if absorbed by a piece of blotting paper." Empty pieces of decorative furniture. What women are supposed to be, as well as those in the subservient class—what Sianne Ngai, in her reading of tone, calls, after Melville, the "Modern Sub-Sub," thinking through Larsen as well, her work as a public librarian, as well as one of Helga Crane's many jobs processing words. The Sub-Sub, the modern submissive and clerical worker, the insignificant subject amid the devouring bureaucratic system. Dora Rosário, like Helga Crane, must beg for money—she must have a blank face, be an empty room—perhaps the novel of the worker, the customer service/clerical class, the contingent teacher, the copyist is marked by being "poised on the edge of an ellipsis." A consciousness filled with spite, irritation, resentment, fury, everything not allowed, impossible, when public facing, because of daring to exist as a mixed-race woman without money or family in the Jim Crow South, as a Catholic widow in the patriarchy of the Salazar dictatorship in Portugal. Sianne Ngai is fascinated with what she characterizes as Helga Crane's Bartelbyan passivity but seems ambivalent about whether this passivity—its atmosphere, its character trait, both, the interior and exterior merging—is radical, a speck of an irritant to overthrow the system. But isn't this what literature is for! To express a solitude in the—at least desired—empty room of one's consciousness, to offer up the ambivalent complexities of the self, to have a face and no face. To write of diminishment in an extravagant way. The opening of *Quicksand*, Helga Crane allowed to be quiet in a quiet room, even though internalizing this always-imagined observer, after the extractive labor of working all day for others, having to obey a rigid set of rules for conduct. Finally relaxing the mask. We realize she will not stay at her job for long once she sits there, unmoving, refusing, not sick exactly but not not sick, a Gregor Samsa in silks. For isn't that the atmosphere of *The Metamorphosis?* Not wanting to go into work, sitting alone in one's room?

She lies in bed, no longer alone in the room. The nurse gazes down at her: at Helga, the Modern Sub-Sub, submerged in "this bog into which she had strayed." She is mired in the quicksand of life as a preacher's wife, her health destroyed by successive pregnancies, her mind revolted by a faith in which she no longer believes. Evening is falling. The novel is ending. Helga Crane will be lost. She will disappear behind the final words, "she began to have her fifth child"—words with a matter-of-fact and neutral tone, a mask that gives nothing away. Motherhood is the final veil, behind which she recedes from view. And if this novel touched us, it was because something had flared out of it for a moment, a vital unwillingness, a darkly brilliant refusal, as arresting and impenetrable as Gregor Samsa's carapace, which, we recalled, is also trashed for the sake of the family, the promise of fertility. Gregor Samsa dies alone, in the night, at the moment when the first light appears behind the window, in a gray hour. Tone, even a gray one, emanates. It is not contained. The tone of *Quicksand* is irritating *to* some readers and energizing *to* us, but in both cases it is *to*. Thinking of this, we reflected that though the variations in interpretations of tone may be too great to call it a "collective" feeling, we might at least call it prepositional. Perhaps the study of tone requires attention to positions and how feeling moves between them. Something is radiating, pulsing, attempting to move across. And it occurred to us that if the tone of a text affects readers in different ways, we should not be surprised, considering how many misunderstandings arise from text messages, emails, and comments on social media, forms of communication on which we depend and that so often plunge us, even among those closest to us, into friction caused by tone. You implied, you insinuated, I felt, to me. To me it appeared this way. A nebulous but insistent charge was flickering from your words. No, I can't prove it. Tone, as in *sound*, stands for the oral, the presence of the speaking body. It indicates what is absent from writing. Tone is the absent presence. It's what writing has instead of timbre: something *indefinite, not clear, vague, subconscious, little, wearing down.* Down or under or to. She closes her eyes. The preposition *sub*, which means "under," can also mean "to" or "toward." *Sub noctem*: toward nightfall.

III

THE WASTELAND, OR OUR OWN
COLORLESS PATCH OF SKY

WE APOLOGIZE for the gap since we reconvened our last meeting of the Committee to Investigate Atmosphere. We haven't been able to find any space to continue our meditations on tone, which we're realizing is also thinking through space. Time has been a blur. Not one year has passed since we've gathered our reflections, like the narrator of W. G. Sebald's *The Rings of Saturn*, but it's impossible, in our vertigo, to actually remember when we last met, here, in this space. (What space are we speaking of, the Google docs, the paragraph, our collected consciousnesses?) We have been doing other forms of labor. We have been occupying other forms of institutional space—the dreaded Zoom box—in meetings and committees, in talks and panels, processing other words, being asked to speak with one voice as if it's only one of us, singular. We are still submerged. The Modern Sub-Sub, *c'est nous?* The unnamed narrator in *The Rings of Saturn* remembers looking out the window while convalescing in the hospital bed in Norwich, in a state of *almost total immobility*, realizing the expanses of his Suffolk summer had shrunk, and all he could stare at was the *colorless patch of sky* in the window covered with a grid of black netting. Staring out at the ugliness of the barren industrial landscape, the multistoried car parks and hospital courtyard, he felt haunted by Kafka's Gregor Samsa, with his dimmed insect eyes, the familiar environs now alien, a *gray wasteland*. Yes, we are still in gray! We wished we were able to move on to another color.

It is mid-February now as we write this, gazing out from different windows, including the artificial light of our computer screens. Our own colorless patch of sky. Something about looking out the window reminds us of our conversation on tone. In her chapter on tone in *Ugly Feelings*, Sianne Ngai attempts to parse feeling from form. And what does this have to do with a landscape? Of tone as a "collective mood"? All these windows collaged over one another. Ours, Sebald's, Gregor Samsa's. What is the collective mood? Something like melancholy and exhaustion. We are never told exactly why the unnamed saturnine narrator is in the hospital and what his walks have allowed him freedom from, but we guess it's overwork, a burnout that also afflicts our traveling salesman Gregor Samsa. There is a reason the narrator moves in his mind to two lecturers in the literature department, who have recently died in their (can it be?) late forties, other selves for the Sebald narrator, who is about the same age. The romantic way their nervous exhaustion and passion is depicted, yet how it dooms them, their intensity for the nineteenth century, the bachelor Swiss literature scholar another one who made exhaustive European walking tours in the off summer months, the Flaubert scholar described like Dürer's angel of melancholy, scribbling on a chair in her office overfilled with notes, the paper like the blankness of snow.

Snow in the streets, the wan luminescence of snowlight through the window blending seamlessly with the pallor of the document, this space where we meet in blanched screen light, where a message invites us to view the changes made in our absence by *all anonymous users*. Though we know our committee is small, we are heartened by the thought that we belong to the crowd of all anonymous users, the untold swarm of those who write in our language, or, expanding further, those who write in any language in the world. Surely translated literature offers a rich field for the study of tone, even if that field is slippery, riddled with sinkholes, and in some places nearly impassable. We recall reading that W. G. Sebald's works revive the Romantic tradition of the long walk, but they restore it as something ghostly and broken, a practice tainted forever by the Holocaust. And undoubtedly we find Sebald's diction subtly archaic, almost courtly, reserved, and suggestive of hidden grief. "In August 1992," he opens *Rings*, "when the dog days were drawing to an end, I set off to walk the county of Suffolk, in the hope of dispelling the emptiness that takes hold of me whenever I have completed a long stint of work." The simple, rustic quality of "when the dog days were drawing to an end," the formality of "in the hope of dispelling"—these are intimations of the reserved, old-world, melancholy tone of Sebald. But of course this is not only Sebald. It is also his translator Michael Hulse, with whom, we have read, Sebald had many battles. Windows collaged over one another: writer and translator struggling, sometimes acrimoniously, toward the collective mood. We open the German book and read, "Im August 1992, als die Hundstage ihrem Ende zugingen, machte ich mich auf eine Fußreise durch die ostenglische Grafschaft Suffolk in der Hoffnung, der nach dem Abschluß einer größeren Arbeit in mir sich ausbreitenden Leere entkommen zu können." We are encouraged by the similarity of the English and German sentences. Though the English version concludes with the recollection of a long stint of work, while German allows the sentence to end with the emptiness the narrator hopes to overcome, the linked clauses share a rhythm. If tone is collective, then it cannot be restricted to a single voice or even a single language. And so, while we are still haunted by the unanswerable question of the senses—is what we call gray the same for all?—we move hesitantly together into the document where a few stray flakes are falling.

Perhaps if tone is something like a collective mood, then reading a translated novel such as *The Rings of Saturn* is something like a communication of voices. Just as we struggle together, in one document, the translator attempts to sound like the original, attempts to listen to something like a strange cadence, that in the case of Sebald sounds like it's from another century, that curious and uncanny tone. For reading Sebald is not reading a singular voice but a library of the past, in the case of *The Rings of Saturn* ventriloquizing the baroque style of Thomas Browne, so perhaps reading Sebald in Michael Hulse's translation is in some ways closer to the "circles of his spiralling prose" originally intended, if we assume that Sebald read Browne and other seventeenth-century writers in English, so that a dubbing or doubling was already occurring (with that we think of Borges, another kindred spirit in the text, on the artifice of dubbing movies, which is also thinking through voice in translation, the uncomfortable chimera in our own consciousness). To attempt to understand the tone in Sebald is something like time traveling—in our investigations of atmosphere, we follow after the vapor trail in front of the window that besets the emptied-out narrator, taking him back centuries, to philosophize the high style of Thomas Browne, an *ars poetica* for his own ghostly voice communicating a spooked consciousness, who sees his world as a shadow of previous centuries:

> His only means of achieving the sublime heights that this endeavour required was a parlous loftiness in his language. In common with other English writers of the seventeenth century, Browne wrote out of the fullness of his erudition, deploying a vast repertoire of quotations and the names of authorities who had gone before, creating complex metaphors and analogies, and constructing labyrinthine sentences that sometimes extend over one or two pages, sentences that resemble processions or a funeral cortège in their sheer ceremonial lavishness.

After Sebald's reading of Robert Burton's *The Anatomy of Melancholy*, we wonder if a melancholy tone might be partially this dizzying series of quotations, the porousness of memory into other epochs. It is perhaps the durational aspect that makes the Sebaldian space melancholy—versus the buoyancy of the anxiety of Walser's long walk. Robert Macfarlane says that the American journey narrative is to discover, the European walk is to recover. Not just a long walk but one that completely empties oneself out, a lengthy rumination through fog, sentences that follow one another in the ceremonial lavishness of a funeral procession, the last page evoking Queen Victoria's funeral, covered in black Mantua silk, draped over mirrors and canvases of landscapes.

Distance makes melancholy. Physical distance: the long walk, the sense of the many hills, roads, and beaches covered and left behind, the funeral procession leading to the grave. Temporal distance: the histories, many of them bleak or appalling, gathered into this text, which feels like a complex reliquary, a cabinet of memento mori, a scrapbook dedicated to the dead. Psychic distance, too: from the first pages, in which the narrator lies immobilized, gazing from his hospital bed at that colorless patch of sky, isolated at such a great height he cannot hear a sound except the wind buffeting the window and the murmur in his own ears, a gulf seems to separate him from the world. As Helga Crane moves in a cloud of irritation, so Sebald's narrator carries distance about with him (we note here the strange intimacy of literature, the way it puts us in contact or even melds us, as we read, with a remote or guarded consciousness). A sense of estrangement shadows his long walk, often emanating from images of verticality that haunt his horizontal progress. The beetle he glimpses swimming across the water in a well—a sight that causes a shudder to go through him. The couple he spies from the top of a cliff, their nude bodies forming a single pale monster, a scene from which he also recoils, remembering the Borges story that calls both mirrors and copulation sinister because they increase the number of human beings. His dream of a labyrinth, seen from above, that illustrates a cross-section of his own brain. The memory of a landscape observed through an airplane window, which causes him to reflect that "if we view ourselves from a great height, it is frightening to realize how little we know about our species, our purpose and our end." If tone involves prepositions, perhaps the tone of *The Rings of Saturn* is *from a great height*—the survivor's position, as the narrator comments in his notes on the Waterloo Panorama: "We, the survivors, see everything from above, see everything at once, and still we do not know how it was." We recall Wayne Koestenbaum's essay "Roberto Bolaño's Tone," which mentions Sebald as a writer with Bolaño's "moral weight," one who exudes something similar (though German) to what a Bolaño character describes as "a certain sadness, a Chilean, bottom-heavy tone." Is this the weight felt in the pit of the stomach as the plane takes off, carrying one into exile, the survivor's country? "Bolaño's supreme accomplishment is his tone," Koestenbaum writes, "if I may hazard such a judgment on a writer I have only read in translation," insisting that tone does filter through a foreign language, perceiving a "haze that floats above Bolaño's fiction," much like a colorless patch of sky, a melancholy to Bolaño's characters, who, like Sebald's, are often nobodies on the verge of disappearance. They are also marked by trauma. "Bolaño's greatness," Koestenbaum writes, "lies in the distance between the horror of the alluded-to event and the imperturbable lucidity of his narrative tone"—what a Bolaño character describes as a 'certain way of expressing opinions, as if from a distance, sadly but gently.'" This tone, this floating haze, is wandering and exilic, the marooned timbre of the literary subaltern. "As Bartleby and his compatriots understood," Koestenbaum writes, "one must leave literature to find it again; one must lower one's voice to raise it."

In *The Rings of Saturn*, Thomas Abrams, the crafter of a model of the Temple of Jerusalem, views his project from a great height. He conducts meticulous research on the Mishnah, Roman architecture, and the edifices of Herod to construct his tiny blocks and columns, with figures a quarter of an inch high, their diminutive scale making them appear as if glimpsed from a mountaintop. Abrams is one of Sebald's moody and solitary obsessives. But he also experiences the magic of his miniature, for the distance effect the model creates in space, its illusion of the bird's-eye view, makes contact with distant time. "When the evening light streams in through this window," he tells the narrator, "and I allow myself to be taken in by the overall view, then I see for a moment the Temple with its antechambers and the living quarters of the priesthood, the Roman garrison, the bath-houses, the market stalls, the sacrificial altars, covered walkways and the booths of the moneylenders, the great gateways and staircases, the forecourts and outer provinces and the mountains in the background, as if everything were already completed and as if I were gazing into eternity." The temple is perhaps also the book. And perhaps the formal diction we observe in Sebald, inspired by the heights Thomas Browne achieved with his loftiness of language, with his ceremonial sentences, resembles the dizzying rows of columns that hold up the temple, a place of ritual. There is no doubt a quality of distance in such stately places. But the temple, like a panorama, also takes in many figures—priests, merchants, moneylenders, soldiers—as a sentence of Thomas Browne takes in the voices of Latin authorities, as a sentence of Sebald takes in Thomas Abrams and Thomas Browne.

In 1610, Galileo was the first to observe the rings of Saturn, raising his telescope to the night sky, although it was only later in the century that astronomers saw that they were a series of small rings with gaps in between and then, centuries later, that each ring was composed of billions of particles, some as minute as grains of sand or as massive as mountains of ice. Perhaps that's how the prose works in *The Rings of Saturn*—by particle, or fragments from these constellations. The uncanny feel to the miniature railway train or temple. Through the voice of Sebald's friend, the prematurely deceased Flaubert scholar scribbling in a corner of her cluttered room, like Dürer's melancholic angel, we learn that for Flaubert a grain of sand in the hem of Emma Bovary's dress could contain the whole of the Sahara. The dizzying collection of objects in *Melencolia I* mirror Thomas Browne's written 1658 catalogue on funeral rites that Sebald lists so lovingly (parataxis as lullaby). The *Wunderkammer*, or wondercabinet. Curiosities: "the circumcision knives of Joshua, the ring which belonged to the mistress of Propertius, an ape of agate, a grasshopper, three-hundred golden bees, a blue opal, silver belt buckles and clasps, combs, iron pins, brass plates and brazen nippers to pull away hair, and a brass jew's-harp that last sounded on the crossing over the black water." Like in the boxes of his fellow miniaturist Joseph Cornell, Sebald's paragraph-collages have a blue tone, like the blue-hour sky. How can this be? We don't know, but we find it to be true that Sebald's pages have a visual beauty to them and that this blue tint is something like their tone. Perhaps, we have wondered, a collage is always melancholy, after Freud's definition, of that which cannot be let go. The passion of the collector, who is always desiring after beauty, even after its shabbiness. Across the scan of our copy of *The Rings of Saturn* a long swirling hair has been left, that was on the photocopier machine. We think of how much Sebald, who loved to copy his images until they achieved the blurriness of the past, would have loved this, a strand of hair swirling across all the pages.

We remember a dinner party at which someone said that the appeal of Sebald's work lay in this inclusion of amateur photographs. Sebald's novels, according to our dinner companion, emerged along with the rise of the digital camera and wonderfully anticipated the smartphone revolution, which has accustomed us all to the poorly lit, indistinct photograph. Once, such images would have been thrown away in disappointment; nowadays we take so many, and it's so tedious to delete them, anyone with a smartphone is guaranteed to be walking around with a pocket full of fuzzy, off-kilter photographs. If our companion of that evening is correct, then perhaps the blue tone of *The*

Rings of Saturn comes from the redemption of inferior objects, the consecration of trash in the *Wunderkammer*, a reverence toward faded, neglected, and discarded things. It occurs to us that this melancholy process of collecting, of not letting go, fundamental to the collage, the photograph album, and the cabinet of curiosities, shares something with the depressive position as described by Melanie Klein and adopted by Eve Kosofsky Sedgwick in her concept of reparative reading. Like Klein's depressive or Sedgwick's reparative reader, Sebald's narrator "tries to organize the fragments and part-objects [he] encounters or creates," filled with an impulse that is "additive and accretive." Perhaps the tone of any private collection is necessarily depressive, reparative, mournful, comforting, blue.

Our Committee to Investigate Atmosphere would like to delicately hypothesize that tone as it operates within Sebald's novels is perhaps something like a filter—there has to be a consistency to it, like a glaze. In Sebald's *The Rings of Saturn*, there is manipulation to give it this effect, to give the landscape, and hence the tone, this deep blue tint, like after Joseph Cornell, with the intention of producing the sensation of a strange dream or fugue state, entering into other epochs. Like grisaille, but also like blue-aille, as Cornell called it. For Sebald, his photographs and postcards—often found in vintage shops, the source unknown—add to the effect of this mournful saturation, like a narrative as a private collection. Perhaps something is sacrificed for this saturnine tone—the tone of the dreamer, the melancholic, the wanderer. The landscape in the present day is surrounded by fog, one of unremitting despair, unlike the loving treasures and historical artifacts of the past. This was Mark Fisher's critique of *The Rings of Saturn*, that he wasn't able to locate the Suffolk landscape that he loved in Sebald's pilgrimage, seeing the work as using the terrain as mere departure for fugue states into past genocides and epochs.

We remember Sianne Ngai's definition of tone as a "global or organizing affect": tone is everywhere, like the gray in grisaille or the blue in blue-aille, and it arranges material. It establishes relations. What are the relations implied in the miniature, the cabinet, the private album? These relations might be reparative, as we suggested, but they also might be aggressive, expressing the hunger for power Susan Sontag perceives in photography, the urge to freeze and shrink reality into collectible items, "consciousness in its acquisitive mood." It is possible to see a totalizing, possessive energy in the desire to reproduce the Temple of Jerusalem in miniature and in the penchant for taking the bird's-eye view, withdrawing from the landscape to such an extent that no detail is visible. We think of the fog that drifts through *The Rings of Saturn*, the endlessly seeping trails of vapor, as if the text has been filtered through a cloud: Thomas Browne's note on the great fog of England in 1674, "the white mist that rises from within a body opened presently after death," Frederick Farrar of Lowestoft regarding the past "through flowing white veils," the "half-fogged mirror" of the Borges story, Michael Hamburger's memory of Berlin and his father's breath, "the white vapor that had carried his words lingering in the ice-cold air." This vapor strikes us as an image not just of the tone of this particular novel but of tone itself.

Perhaps tone is what colors an atmosphere. Does distance have a color? Yes, we realize, it has two colors: gray and blue. Distance lessens the contrast between colors, so that they can appear to fade and move toward gray, the boundaries between shapes diminishing, an effect achieved by Dürer, we read in a description of his woodcuts, by the use of fine lines to depict far-off objects such as mountains. This attenuation of line strikes us as homologous with the blending of voices in Sebald's work. Sebald, too, employs an aerial perspective that thins borders, and the description of Dürer's art we are reading reminds us of *The Rings of Saturn*, which also "suggest[s] atmospheric perspective within . . . vast vistas." We turn to the note on aerial perspective in Leonardo da Vinci's *Treatise on Painting*, like Browne's *Urn Burial* a text of the seventeenth century, where we read, in John F. Rigaud's translation, "The air, between the eye and the object seen, will change the color of that object into its own; so will the azure of the air change the distant mountains into blue masses." To create a distance effect, the artist advises, paint your objects increasingly bluer and less distinct. We hypothesize that this evocation of distance gives Cornell's blue-aille its deep saturation of nostalgia. But we also read that looking through fog or "thick air" will make distant things appear larger, rather than smaller, which prompts us to reconsider once more the object relations of *The Rings of Saturn*, suspecting that they can't be reduced to a one-way process, that the novel's aerial view, crossed by waves of turbid air, may enlarge things as much as it shrinks them, and that this unexpectedly enlarging perspective, which makes things appear overwhelming in size, may be indicated by the grain of sand in which Flaubert perceived the Sahara. Dust, rather than fog, may organize the tone of this novel of particles. We recall the "mealy dust" that obscures the narrator's vision during the onset of a devastating hurricane and, afterward, the "pollen-fine dust that hung for a long time in the air," a floating, granular substance, occupying the smallest and largest scales. This is the dust of the wasteland, the end of the world. The looming threat of this ultimate acquisition, when everything will be miniaturized, pulverized, and collected by devastation, haunts every effort at repair. In dreams, the narrator remarks, one sees through "something nebulous, gauze-like," a veil through which "a handful of dust is a desert."

Somehow after all of this, months later, now in late May, we are back in the fog or vapor, in our quest, perhaps quixotic, to investigate atmosphere via committee. We have grasped this tonality of melancholy as a way to understand a certain gaze or tint that clouds over a text. And there is an elegiac spirit to *The Rings of Saturn*, as well as other companion texts, such as Mark Fisher's and Justin Barton's 2013 audio-essay *On Vanishing Land*, their collective walk through Suffolk, which begins at the "unvisited vastness" of the Felixtowe container port and ends at Sutton Hoo, the site of an Anglo-Saxon ship burial, considering the disorienting effects of the horizon. It is here that the atmospheric is bound up in considerations of place and the local, which the committee has already suspected, what Fisher has said he longed for in Sebald's Suffolk tour, channeling the ghost stories of M. R. James that took place there, and both slowing down and layering time. Not a fugue state, which is what Fisher criticizes in Sebald, but something acoustic, atmospheric, like the ambient electronic music that punctuates each section and the tenor of Barton's voiceover. The depth of Brian Eno's composition "Ambient 4: On Land," which inspires the name for the piece, something like the pretty and pastoral as overtones, but underneath there's a dissonance, an emotional undoing. Here—somewhere—we think, as we listen to the audio essay, is tone. It is a rarefied air, we are back to the nineteenth century, but we are also being haunted by our current landscape. The feel of this is more of the eerie, as Fisher theorizes, a calmness, almost a silence, except for the ecstatic music and solemn voiceover. The eerie is outside, in the atmosphere, in the partially unpeopled landscape. The fog surrounding is that of a mystery, writes Fisher. What happened to create these ruins, these abandoned structures of capitalism? What caused their disappearance?

We wonder what this means, if a tone of eeriness is closest to silence. Perhaps we are thinking of sound in *On Vanishing Land* and other more polyvocal texts, as opposed to the ubiquitous "voice." Perhaps this sound or silence is what's closest to tone. When thinking through Amiri Baraka's poetry, Fred Moten has distinguished between "voice" and "sound," which is useful for our efforts here. Moten says, in an interview:

> I always thought that "the voice" was meant to indicate a
> kind of genuine, authentic, absolute individuation, which
> struck me as (a) undesirable and (b) impossible. . . . Whereas

a "sound" was really within the midst of this intense engagement with everything: with all the noise that you've ever heard, you struggle somehow to make a difference, so to speak, within that noise. And that difference isn't necessarily about you as an individual, it's much more simply about trying to augment and to differentiate what's around you. And that's what a sound is for me.

We are inspired here, as the Committee to Investigate Atmosphere, by Fred Moten's thinking of poetry as sound that engages with everything—the inside meets the outside—an echo away from the individual concept of voice, the product of capitalism, much as in his collaborative efforts with Stefano Harney, which take place in books, in interviews, on walks, in the space they call the undercommons. We are entranced by this project of "we," such as in these works and in *On Vanishing Land*, and the atmosphere it evokes, both trancelike meditation and manifesto. It was on a slow walk overlooking the Hudson at the end of April, a rare time together in a landscape, that we have renewed our interest in this work, this work of the we, this conversation that is about combining voices, trying to find tone, thinking beyond the individual I. We felt a desire to somehow commune with each other, and with ghosts of the past, and find a way to travel through time. That is what literature has been to us, both together and separately, an atmospheric commons or an undercommons. We think together, read together, write together, in a way to find language for a historical intimacy, an intimacy of the past and present. In this way, we are hoping for this entry into tone to be a course of study as Moten has defined it, in an interview with Harney:

> We are committed to the idea that study is what you do with other people. It's talking and walking around with other people, working, dancing, suffering, some irreducible convergence of all three, held under the name of speculative practice. The notion of a rehearsal—being in a kind of workshop, playing in a band, in a jam session, or old men sitting on a porch, or people working together in a factory—there are these various modes of activity. The point of calling it "study" is to mark that the incessant and irreversible intellectuality of these activities is already present.

We are drawn to the idea of a speculative practice in plural, like the unreality of the wanderings on the Dunwich heath later on in Sebald's tour, finally finding himself on the outskirts of Middleton, being served tea in Michael Hamburger's garden, and slowly finding the "I" dissolved into "we" as he considers his moldy manuscripts and notebooks, and looking over at his heavy table in his studio, overlooking a north-facing window, he imagines both of them together, writing at their desks, considering quitting academia, a sense of strangeness, in this becoming we, that marks, perhaps, one of the aspects of tone in the novel. It is we who have lost our grip on reality, he writes, in a disorienting passage, when we are so engrossed in this work, that we lose sense of the borders between space and time. Elsewhere we have described Sebald's magic act of becoming others as ventriloquism, inspired, we know, by Thomas Bernhard's digressive acts of dialogue, punctuated only rarely by a tag of attribution, so that the he blurs into an I blurs into a we. Sebald, in an elegiac or melancholy register to Bernhard's paranoia, or Walser's anxiety, asks: "Across what distances of time do the elective affinities and correspondences connect? How is it that one perceives oneself in another human being, or, if not oneself, then one's own precursor?" We will end this second movement of our investigations wondering whether it is the tones laid over one another that produce atmosphere and whether there is something to this effect that we might term both ecological and historical.

IV

HOARD, OR AN UNAIRED ROOM

OUR COMMITTEE reconvened at the beginning of summer, as the rats multiplied and mushrooms sprang up under the trees. The corner of the couch where we habitually worked grew hot and musty, infused with a thick but not unpleasant smell of paper, the exhalation of the notebooks and paperbacks gathered in bags and piles around us, a collection that grows no matter how often we cut it back. Here we read Dodie Bellamy's essay "Hoarding as *Écriture*," from *Bee Reaved*, a collection published after the death of the writer Kevin Killian, Bellamy's partner of thirty-three years, a book of loss and grief, of widowhood and dying creatures, of a breathless, hungry, associative energy. It seems to us that a hoard, with its power to create an atmosphere, to infiltrate and surround, at once possessing and possessed, must have a relation to tone. Perhaps a hoard *is* a tone—the writing, Bellamy suggests, of excess and shame. We find ourselves drawn to the shape of this writing on the

page, each paragraph surrounded by white space, like a room
or box, like the boxes of ephemera Bellamy and Killian donate
to the Beinecke Library at Yale in the first sentence of the
essay, clearing a space in their one-bedroom apartment, and
also, it occurs to us, like the paragraph blocks we have been
writing, both alone and together, for some time. What is the
appeal of these boxes of text? A sense of excitement, of juxta-
position, of never knowing what one will come across next, the
leaps of thought, Bellamy's essay cramming together photographs gelatin Henry James kefir genetics the death of a
beloved cat. Euphoria of permission. A trance state. Let it all
in. And then the tension of not knowing where it will end.
"When is enough enough?" Bellamy's essay concludes with the
Gigogne tumblers by Duralex she buys on Amazon, enamored
by their roundness. "I lift one to my mouth and suck," she
writes. "Glass as tit." These "curvaceous breast glasses" evoke
a lost mother, "that painful wrenching apart," and a tragic
view of language, the "stacks and stacks of words" that can
never close the gap between self and other, self and world.

The tone of the hoard, despite its lushness (because of it?), may
be a tone of despair. Those Amazon tumblers remind us of
Heike Geissler's *Seasonal Associate*, a collaboration with the
translator Katy Derbyshire, which recounts a stint of work at
an Amazon distribution center in Leipzig. This text is narrated
by an I describing the experience of a You who has taken on
this job out of desperation. "From now on," the reader is warned
on the first page, "you are me." You, the reader, are a writer,
translator, and mother, desperate for work. You make your way

to the dispatch hall on the outskirts of the city, passing office complexes, brothels, gas stations, and housing projects, places tinted and tainted by their distance from the city center, their poverty and lack of prospects, like rows of cardboard boxes. Maybe tone is global distribution: a generator of itself. An insistent odor. As You sit waiting for an interview (we are capitalizing You as the name of a character here), You can smell "the stench of unwashed laundry or of laundry hung out to dry in an unaired room."

As we sit thinking of tone as an unaired room, on the perpetual couch, our tit now actually in the mouth of a sick and sleeping baby, the stuffy living area making us both sweaty and shivering, much like the You in the body of the city that is a distribution center, its blasts of warm steam, in Heike Geissler's *Seasonal Associate*, we strain our neck to find the galley we have behind us on the Semiotext(e) shelf, like Gerhard Richter's painting of his daughter on the cover of the English translation. Our gray couch came in a series of boxes and had to be assembled, and we had hope at the time that it would transform our space into something more homey, always that desire when the boxes and boxes come, that finally we have bought something that can make us feel something, but instead, when assembled, it reminded us of a shabby waiting area, much like the purgatorial space where You sit waiting for an interview, unable to breathe, noticing the dust on the leaves of the plants. There is an *unheimlich* feeling to such corporate spaces that attempt to create hominess while at work that causes your home to feel alien even from yourself, and the exhaustion of such constant airlessness makes your body too enervated to find pleasure while at home or even to perform the maintenance labor on your self or your space.

No one's in the apartment. You already miss your desk, even though you're standing right next to it. You go to the bedroom and hang up socks on the drying rack. You're slow, as though in a land consisting only of stretching time that fills itself.

The committee wonders whether, in texts like *Seasonal Associate* or the kindred Hiroko Oyamada's *The Factory*, work itself can be described as an atmosphere and what this also has to do with the hoarding impulse we are investigating. Work is an embodied anxiety and queasiness that absents the self (the "matter of life and death" referred to in the opening line of *Seasonal Associate*). One is never alone anymore, when thinking of work, when being at work, especially in the distribution center as teeming polluted city (distribution center as a monster body, You are in its mouth), where it's impossible to even pretend one can walk around, grab a coffee, be alone with one's thoughts, fully leave. "Work simply alters its own physical state, going from a solid to a gas and entering your body through your nose after the actual end of the work, circulating inside you." In the distribution center, You are being distributed, You are multiple, You are the horde, You are never alone. Anything can be sold, processed, distributed, including yourself. What is distributed are bad feelings—shame, despair, constant precarity and financial anxiety, the sick feelings of being a kindergartener on their perpetual first day, as Geissler describes, only partially soothed by the accumulation of paychecks and of course the accrual of things, the only way to feel anything through shame and despair under late-stage capitalism. The You narrator in *Seasonal Associate* confesses to feeling a vibrational intensity toward the accumulation of objects in this fulfillment center, perhaps like the sparks of the "contingent tableau" Jane Bennett describes in *Vibrant Matter*, her meditation on the political and erotic ecology of things, and Dodie Bellamy's ecstatic assemblage in Amazon boxes. There is the gear pack of swag given on the first day that reminds the narrator of the college welcome bag, like the branded knickknacks on the dystopian workplace television show *Severance*, collected as prizes to foster competitive teamwork. The narrator feels pulses of pleasure and affect for stock and its spectacle—for its organization and structure within the dizzying labyrinth, for even the moments of mess and disarray, being out of order, of packages falling and spilling. "You see a dust-coated stock museum; you like it." The stock is more alive than the human zoo managing it—the stock falls asleep in its rooms and neighborhoods. We wonder whether the tone is not only distribution but also fulfillment center—and, if so, what is it fulfilling?

The hoard is never full. It is a surfeit that alchemizes instantly into lack. Both noun and verb, "hoard" designates both process and product. In its self-generating liveliness, a hoard is similar to a collection, but unlike the collection, the hoard is characterized by loss of value. We notice the distinction in the tone and affective landscape of these novels depending on the arrangement of material, Sebald's refined lists of Thomas Browne's *Wunderkammer* treasures versus the rotting pile, the hoard. Items in a collection are lovingly arranged and displayed, each with its own particular place and meaning. Browne's list of things from the probably imaginary Musaeum Clausum is a "register of marvels," Sebald writes: medals, coins, and fabulous curiosities, including "a precious stone from a vulture's head" and "astonishing writings and artworks," such as a supposedly lost poem in the Getick language wrapped in wax. These items have been curated; they receive care. Browne's museum is *clausum*: closed. The hoard, by contrast, is expansive and composed of things that have lost their value, things made with the purpose of losing their value, like the baseball cap Geissler's You packs for Amazon, "that already looks so lived-in it could hardly get more worn." This cap is "nothing but a ragged piece of cloth, more like something for adherents to a radicalized acceleration of the commodity cycle, people who only buy what has to be thrown away because it fails to meet its requirements as a usable product, serves only to move money and material." The strange, apparently unnecessary *more like* in this sentence—why say the cap is *more like* something and then describe precisely what it is?—strikes us as a hoard sign, the English *more like*, the German *eher* (rather) instigating a doubling, an expansion of the object beyond itself. *More like / eher* conjures another cap, a spectral twin of this one, which will also have its own twin, in a never-ending excretion. The cap, like the hoard, infects the space around it: "You almost sense the greasy feel of sweat mixed with dust." It's disgusting, yet it also exerts a weird garbage-attraction, or what Jane Bennett calls "thing-power." "You're tempted to try it on for a moment," Geissler writes, "perhaps because it looks like something you found on the street for which you might have some use." It looks, again, like something else: not a twin this time but an alternative version, something discovered elsewhere, away from here. If it wasn't new, being packed in a box in the bowels of the distribution center, if You found it outside on the street, it might have value. We are struck by the similarity of this imagined meeting between You and the cap to Jane Bennett's epiphanic encounter with a trash tableau on a Baltimore street: "one large men's black plastic work glove, one dense mat of oak pollen, one unblemished dead rat, one white plastic bottle cap, one smooth stick of wood." Discarded, useless things. "I stood enchanted," Bennett writes—a feeling Geissler's You also seems to experience, for a moment, but only while picturing the cap truly old, not merely fake old, and not here, being packed in the distribution center, but on the street. Outside, it might be desirable. But here, no. And for both the cap and You, there's no outside. You're inside with the cap, twinned with it, in the hoard. "It's because of all the things that are here, which someone or another wants to buy, that you're here in the first place."

The You in *Seasonal Associate* is consumed with thing-power or, at least, thing-attraction, which is close to thing-ambivalence. Geissler notes the use of the corporate and American term "tote" for the receptacles where things are stored, things are moved around, things are cataloged and processed, and she notes its closeness to the German word for death. We are reading a *Totenbuch*; the lists of the dead are the seemingly useless and uncanny items that are ordered out of some need, some lack that can never be filled. We think about Lauren Berlant's concept of "slow death" and wonder whether it can be applied not only to the You of the novel and the other mechanized and exhausted workers but also to the dizzying and already decaying field of things. Sometimes there is a surreality to this assemblage, or at least to the processing of these things as words, of the things that appear in the death tote—to the "aquariums and luminous globes," the celebrity mugs, the children's medical kits as miniatures. There is, You realizes, every form of thing in existence, cheap fashion, plastic kitsch, that exists forever, in its degraded form, but is only useful momentarily, in fact often forgotten when it arrives, so often returned battered and worn. We look at our tote and realize it's almost empty. We are writing in this room while shivering and sweaty in our bed, having now caught the familial virus. We feel lucky that it is summer, that we don't have to work sick, as is so often the expectation, or deal with the bureaucratic surveillance that the You narrator undergoes in *Seasonal Associate*, the smarm of the male doctor and manager, the expectation of the sick note, the internalized worry that she is somehow faking it. But she is faking nothing, except that her body is not worn down, the deterioration that Berlant describes in their essay on slow death, borrowing from David Harvey's positing that to be sick, under capitalism, is to be unable to work. All the You narrator wants to be is slow amid the expectations of a mechanized and cheerful speed. She looks for corners in the distribution center, on the train, in order to be slow, which is to think, and then ultimately is sick and unable to work. Once You is home, sick, the schismed narrator I, while window-shopping in Munich, reflects on the desire for money, for more money, which would bring happiness, through shopping for luxury goods, like the Duralex tumblers as teat. What Geissler is describing here presciently anticipates the pandemic, the Instagram aesthetic of coziness, all of which promises a home, a room, a place to escape, to arrive at Berlant's "good life," which never arrives, but what does arrive are the Amazon trucks outside on the street, the boxes at your door:

> you suddenly understand the cocooning phenomenon, albeit not for long, and you also understand ambitious all-day home-cooking sessions, collecting travel catalogs, dreaming of the future, upgrading home interiors, wallpapering with soft carpets, you understand blankets with arm holes, fur-lined slippers, housecoats, morning home clothing, noon home clothing, evening home clothing, reading circles, corner sofas, evenings in front of the TV.

As we consider the arrangements that seem to produce tone, the relationships and organization of things, it strikes us that the preposition we would associate with Geissler's novel is *inside*. Indoors in summer, quarantined, still caring for a sick child, we continue to pick at this thing-ambivalence, the shifting attitude toward things in Geissler's text, which seems to be written from inside the hoard. The desire for a cocoon of things reminds us of Jill, a woman featured on the *Hoarders* television show and described in Jane Bennett's essay "Powers of the Hoard." A friend of Jill's, explaining why Jill resists having spoiled food taken from her refrigerator, tells the cleaners, "to her it felt like you removed layers of skin." One is enveloped in the hoard, as in the wearable blankets and fuzzy slippers of *Seasonal Associate*, becoming attached even to the stench of the rapidly putrefying good life. One identifies with the hoard and is hoarded by it. Working at the Amazon distribution center takes the narrator deep inside the supply chain of the craving for things, so far inside that she finds herself at one with things, while still desiring them, as if queasily turning inside out. From inside, it's hard to tell where the surface is. Borders dissolve. "You're one of them now, you see," the I-narrator tells You, referring to the defeated-looking people waiting in the entrance hall, "even though you see it differently and will say all sorts of things to emphasize that there's a distance between you and the other employees and especially between you and the company— but that's not true. You're now in the mouth of the company (in its jaws?) and are being predigested before you're allowed to enter the rest of the digestive tract." In the belly of the distribution center, there is no distance. In this sense, the tone of hoarding, while related to the tone of collecting, may in fact be its opposite. Distance, the ability to stand outside and take an overview, is essential to collecting. We recall Susan Stewart's description of the collection as a system of objects within a larger capitalist economy, one "designed to serve as a stay against the frailties of the very monetary system from which it has sprung." For Stewart, the collection carves out a space of meaning opposed to the brutal transformation of labor into exchange value. This gives the collection its "aura of transcendence and independence"—one that, she adds, "is symptomatic of the middle class's values regarding personality." Not so the hoard. This is the place of downward mobility, where, Kevin Vennemann points out in the afterword to *Seasonal Associate*, the narrator is addressed in the original German as *du*, the pronoun for intimates, rather than the more respectful and professional *Sie*. "We all use *du* around here," her team leader says—a pretense of equality. But, Vennemann writes, "entirely bereft of its secondary functionalities as an indicator of warmth, family, friendship, proximity, the *du* has been reduced to its passive-aggressive and dehumanizing implications." We think of the scene in Hiroko Oyamada's *The Factory*, another novel of work on the inside, when one of the narrators, Yoshiko Ushiyama, meets her brother's girlfriend, a temp agent who has arranged for the brother to work, like Yoshiko, in the city's enormous factory. Very soon, the girlfriend begins addressing Yoshiko, with exaggerated familiarity, as "Yoshiko-chan," as if speaking to a child. "Now she's calling me Yoshiko-*chan*?" Yoshiko thinks. "I felt like an iguana was crawling around my insides." The nausea of absorption, of the basement where Yoshiko works, with its "muffled, manmade air," of the voracious factory that swallows everything around it, until it contains even mountains, forests, a massive river, an ocean. It's the resistance to being devoured, Kevin Vennemann surmises, that causes Geissler's I-narrator to address the You in the novel as *Sie*—a decision that seems peculiar at first, since this You, working at Amazon, is presumably the former self of I. It would make sense to address oneself with the intimacy of *du*. The use of *Sie* opens a strange distance in the narrator's relationship with herself. A distance, Vennemann writes, "of humanity-affirming formality." A distance that, in the hoard, must be fought for.

The hoard is inside, a way to store up, to attempt to survive the constancy of atmospheric precarity. As Berlant writes in their introduction to *Cruel Optimism*, "Fantasy is the means by which people hoard idealizing theories and tableaux about how they and the world 'add up to something.'" In the proletariat spatial regime of *Seasonal Associate* and *The Factory*, the main characters are not Main Characters but workers constantly kept on the outside—they work as much as anyone else, except for not being paid for their lunch hours. They are temporary, no one speaks to them, isolated by partitions at cubicles to increase productivity, sometimes they are not even given a uniform, or their shabby uniform segregates them from the real workers, the imagined and fictional community or family. An entire warehouse or factory of workers who are not really there, and have convinced themselves that they are only passing through, that if they work hard enough, they will get to the next level, that it's not permanent, that they still have their youth, until they do not. The unnamed brother of Yoshiko Ushiyama, a redundant systems engineer who has taken temporary employment proofing absurd manuals such as the booklet *Goodbye to All Your Problems and Mine: A Guide to Mental Health Care*, illustrated with two smiling meatballs, takes to eating chocolates and sweets at his desk and falling asleep regularly there. He soon learns that the good life the factory promises is just a fantasy—he doesn't have time to make it to the other side, where there is the river, restaurants, cafeterias with better food, as opposed to the reheated leftovers they are expected to bring, the promised land of the factory and its natural settings closed to outsiders. "What happens when those fantasies start to fray—depression, dissociation, pragmatism, cynicism, optimism, activism, or an incoherent mash?" Berlant asks. The three alternating characters are stuck in what Berlant calls an impasse, a stretching out of time, existing only in the present, which they cannot move forward. We learn it's been fifteen years since Yoshio Furufue lived there, having no idea why he's there, becoming like the moss he's studying, unsure what genre he's stuck in. We realize that these novels of precarity and impasse experience a crisis or confusion of genre, as do their characters. How long have they been at the factory? What does the factory make? What is their purpose there? Are they in a cozy or awkward workplace sitcom, a mystery, a dystopian spectacle, a melodrama, a detective story? We notice that it is often put forward, as a criticism, that a tone is aesthetically inconsistent, but Berlant suggests that this genre crisis is itself the crisis of the ordinariness of precarity and of awkwardness. The disorientation, in terms of the time shifts, the POV switches, are part of the affective atmosphere that is both present and strange. We find it compelling, in considering both *Seasonal Associate* and *The Factory*—the latter takes place entirely on location; even in the case of the tenured bryologist, he lives on campus—that there are scenes of walking that resist any release of the European walker or flaneur, because of the uncanniness of these spaces, the *Unheimlichkeit* of the work campus as town or city. (They have everything but the cemetery, we are told in *The Factory*; we wonder why this is.)

Perhaps the absence of a cemetery at the factory gestures toward the lack of any possible escape or ending, the cruel eternity of the impasse. The hoard is a key image in *Cruel Optimism*, especially in Berlant's reading of Charles Johnson's story "Exchange Value," which turns on the moment when two impoverished Black boys break into their dead neighbor's apartment and discover a reeking pile of cash and things. One of the boys goes on an immediate and miserable spending spree; Berlant notes his purchase of "ugly, badly-made, expensive clothes that shame him right away," the meat he eats "until he gets sick." We think of Geissler's narrator in the distribution center, rushing for her lunch break, "in a jumble of people, where it's impossible not to be touched," through a hallway that "spits out" the employees for their break, the eagerly awaited lunch prefaced by the image of spewing. "You eat," the I-narrator tells her avatar, "and soon you'll be gobbling your food down." The longer she stays at the center, the faster she eats, her body mirroring the driving circulation of capitalism against which, for Berlant, the hoard is a persistent if paralyzing fantasy. Possessing a hoard, Berlant argues, seems like what anybody would want, but the sovereignty granted by the hoard cuts the owner off from circulation and therefore from life, so that the promised satisfaction becomes intolerable, "a nightmarish burden, a psychotic loneliness, and just tainted." How does the impasse operate when one is not the owner of the hoard but an insignificant item inside it? To put it another way, we might ask, with Yoshiko Ushiyama in *The Factory*, "why all the offal?" In the restaurant near the factory, workers are served an abundance of internal organs: liver, tongue, and tripe. Tiny Itsumi, a woman of unguessable age with unreal-looking, "unnaturally straight" hair, grills the food at the table, scolding the others for touching their food with chopsticks that have been contaminated by raw meat. "Raw blood will make you sick." Weird conviviality of the factory, overly familiar motherliness of Itsumi, cringe-inducing pet names, tripe that threatens to come up again as soon as it's swallowed, a chunk of liver tossed in a mouth, liver that turns out to be still frozen. There's lots of food, but it all seems somehow inedible. Why all the offal? Is it a metaphor for the state of the workers, organs inside the factory? Are these oneiric meal scenes meant to demonstrate how the factory eviscerates its workers or how they are invited, at its hundreds of eateries, to devour their own insides? Or is the offal a species of joke, a play on the gargantuan expansiveness of the factory, whose extent in space cannot be measured any more than the length of Itsumi's lifetime ("I never found out how old Itsumi was," Ushiyama comments at the end of the dinner scene)—as if to say, what else do you expect to eat in here? This is the place of internalized estrangement, of interned aliens, of interminable internship. We are all outsiders here, where there is no Outside. Such heavy, overburdened metaphors. Impacted imagery. We remember the description of the boy in "Exchange Value," which we read about in Berlant's book, giving some spare change to his elderly neighbor, the keeper of the hoard, who "puts it in her mouth and eats it."

The Committee to Investigate Atmosphere takes seriously Berlant's theory that "affective atmospheres are shared, not solitary, and that bodies are continuously busy judging their environments and responding to the atmospheres in which they find themselves." Nowhere for Berlant is this hoarding desire more intense than in terms of an ambivalent relationship to food. Even when eating alone, this is the texture of the social at the factory, even talking about food, or not having food, like the scientist Furufue and Yoshiko, who share an awkward meal of soba noodles at the end of the book, Furufue's access to the factory's restaurant displaying his elite status and belonging versus her outsiderness yet also their shared alienation and, toward the end, their becoming nonhuman. The minor characters and coworkers in Oyamada's novel often gorge themselves in a borderless way that revolts these two narrators, their unruly and grotesque bodies, after Bakhtin on Rabelais, sucking down cafeteria fare or uncooked bar meat as if it were a feast. These middle-management workers are working themselves to death, and food becomes a form of pleasure, their time, their lunchtime, their time after work, a way to reproduce their exhausted labor. "Eating is *their* time. It's their *time*," writes Lauren Berlant in "Two Girls, Fat and Thin," their close reading of Mary Gaitskill's novel that also switches and blurs points of view. Finding ourselves at an impasse, gesturing toward an ending, we attempt a list of food pleasures and discourses in *The Factory* like Berlant performs in "Two Girls, Fat and Thin," a partial list that is its own hoard, that piles on, an excessive banquet:

"A bowl of miso soup—the one with no pork" . . . "a giant slab of tonkatsu, stir-fried eggplant and pork liver, an extra large helping of rice, natto, and seven umeboshi from the condiment island" . . . "digging in . . . " "shoveling" "slurping it down"; "Thousand Island dressing on the shredded cabbage that came with his tonkatsu" . . . "took the cabbage off his plate, pink with dressing, put it on his rice, then crammed it into his mouth. Setting his chopsticks down for a moment, he stuck an umeboshi in his mouth, sucked on the flesh, cracked the stone with his molars, and tongued free the innermost kernel before spitting it back onto his plate" . . . "Then I watched my advisor cover his natto in mustard, pour some soy sauce on top, and dump the whole thing over the last of his rice" . . . "thick strings of natto"; "I bit into the hard shell and soft chocolate filled my mouth"; "listened to them talking about some barbecue"; "Now that we had our drinks, everyone grabbed a paper bib and put it on. The bibs said MOO-MOO YAKINIKU and had a cartoon cow on them"; "Before long, a big plate full of assorted meats came, with a side of kimchi"; "bits of liver, tongue, and tripe on the grill"; "You can have soba, steak, ramen, fried chicken, fast food. In the hotel, we've got French, Italian, sushi, teppanyaki"; "So what did you bring for lunch?"; "All I could find was two energy bars and a bottle of tea" . . . "a tangerine" . . . "one of those hard candies with the chocolate filling"; "Irinoi and Glasses both grabbed pieces of gum out of the containers on their desks and started chewing." "The growing collection of goodies on my desk" . . . "How nice. Look at all those snacks"; "Itsumi and the Captain switched to shochu. I ordered a lemon sour." "Chopsticks in hand" . . . "another dish of kimchi" . . . "I think I'm ready for noodles." "I want the bibimbap, but not the stone-roasted one, the other one." "Noodles, too, and another lemon sour"; "five chocolate croissants"; "the pickled plum and shiso cutlet with fried shrimp set" . . . "the special pork loin" . . . "the fillet cutlet"; "My brother ripped through his pork, barely bothering to chew." "Her plum and shiso cutlet came with a little saucer of ponzu with grated radish in it. She picked up her chopsticks, scraped the tartar sauce from the shrimp onto her plate"; "purple pickles" . . . "can I get some more cabbage?" . . . "she started dipping her pork in the ponzu. She took a bite, added more sauce and took another bite, even though it already had an umeboshi inside"; " 'Personally, I enjoy the, uh, croquette.' . . . 'What is it? Koban croquette?' " . . . " 'Waraji.' " " 'Waraji croquette?' " " 'The waraji croquette lunch special. With ground beef inside. It's sweet and spicy. You'll love it!' " "It's not ground beef though. It's pulled beef cooked in sweet sauce." "Grilled fish with rice and miso, an omelet with a side of toast." "We've got a great dim sum stand, a French creperie, a vegetable tanmen place, and a really good BBQ spot for dining alone. We've even got an eel restaurant that delivers anywhere. I've eaten broiled eel on rice in the middle of the forest"; "Something metallic clanked against the receiver. Probably a can of coffee. They say you'll get diabetes if you drink too much of that stuff"; "I'd ordered coffee with whipped cream, but by the time I tried to take a sip, the cream had already melted, and I was left with a normal bitter cafe au lait. I thought about sweetening it, but didn't know where to find the sugar"; "A slice of cheesecake"; "These pickles are really something" . . . "bowl of soba" . . . "gnawing on a spare rib" . . . "Looking over the handwritten menu, I was almost happy. *Lunch Specials Soki Soba Set—Goya Champloo Set—Tempura Set (Squid and Seasonal Fish)—Daily Special. Sets may include: vegetables, rice, noodles, miso soup.*" "The special today is fuirichi with a side of rafute"; "I looked inside my bowl. Thick yellow noodles and pork in a clear, almost colorless broth. Green onions and pink pickles on top."

Although there's something pleasurable about all of these units of foods hoarded together, we wonder what this has to do with our understanding of tone as a shared affective atmosphere. We consider the strange modularity of *The Factory*. Oyamada's translator David Boyd describes her method of composition: "In her own words, she writes in 'blocks,' discrete units of text, without much consideration for how each piece will eventually fit in with the rest of the story." The combination of units creates the vertiginous, slippery movement of *The Factory*, the "jump cuts" Parul Sehgal identifies in her review of the novel, the "scenes that dissolve mid-paragraph and flow into the next without so much as a line break." Oyamada's blocks remind us of both Bellamy's text boxes and Geissler's paragraphs, often solid rectangles, without quotation marks, where voices run together, perhaps a form well suited to the writing of the hoard: these overflowing receptacles, their borders pressured and splitting from within. Such uncontainable writing recalls the research of Janine Dakyns, Sebald's Flaubert scholar in *The Rings of Saturn*, whose papers have covered her floor, walls, and furniture, forcing her into a single chair in the middle of the room. Janine might easily be described as a hoarder. Yet what a different tone suffuses her "virtual paper landscape," with its mountains, valleys, and glaciers, its gentle glow at dusk "like snow in the fields, long ago," from the "dreary and outdated and banal" atmosphere of Amazon—originally, of course, a bookseller—and the dusty smell of old paper in the factory. Janine's floods of paper can still evoke beauty, a rarefied existence, and even "a perfect kind of order," for she knows where everything is. Her life, though cluttered, is a writing life. But *Seasonal Associate* and *The Factory* take place in the world of production, including the production of literature. The two Ushiyamas, brother and sister, work at either end of a mysterious chain of publishing, the brother editing nonsensical documents (words mashed together, "When my brother finishes cosmetologo111001 in the south were many black . . ."), the sister, on the disposal end, shredding paper for up to nine hours a day. This is literature as a meaningless burden, words blurring before the brother's eyes, "squiggles and dots, symbols and patterns, running on endlessly." While Geissler's I-narrator at Amazon receives a shock: she finds herself holding a book by a man she knows, a former friend. She packs his books, pulling on her fleece hood in the freezing stream of air from a gate that won't close, where her requests for the gate to be fixed will provoke a reprimand from the company, saying they refuse to bring her a heater, and she will no longer have the strength to explain the misunderstanding. She will just tremble. She handles the work by the man who is called a successful writer. "There in the dispatch hall, where I placed approximately forty of his books in the crate for preordered products—meaning I knew what people would read and what they considered a good Christmas gift—it was as if I were the chambermaid and he were the guest. It was as if we were showing our true faces."

We find ourselves opening and opening this inquiry, this atmosphere we share together, needing to keep adding one last note or thought before closing this section, which seems appropriate for an inquiry into the aesthetics of the hoard. The pleasure we feel moving around our own boxes of text, the space we occupy, not having to worry (yet) about how this text will exist as a physical object, as content, as a book to move, to be moved, and then not to move. We are Heike Geissler's You, or are we Heike Geissler's I, in love with books, in love with books and books, still allowing ourselves to exist in that pure and speculative space of literature. We lie on our couches, books and notebooks spread all over our bodies like the Flaubert scholar mirroring Dürer's hoarding angel of melancholy, piling on books upon books, having them exist together, in the collectivity of the minor literature, not caring about their sales rank or whether they're recommended in the algorithm or whether they are "successful" by market dictates or whether the book will "land with readers." An alienating realization, for You to realize laboring in the underworld of book production, that publishing, that the modes of production, that the modes of distribution that push out books by the millions, has nothing to do with actual literature, with that borderless act of writing and reading and writing what one is reading. Yet all attachments are optimistic, Berlant tells us, and we listen. It is, after all, a book that releases You from the distribution center, in a moment of strange sorcery, when the I-narrator reaches into the past to make contact with You through a book "I've put in your box." The book was never in an Amazon box—it's out of print, the I-narrator admits—but still, she has placed it there for You to find "like a hidden treasure." It is a utopian text about an architect who built a university campus but didn't include any paths. Instead, the architect allowed the students to tread their own trails in the winter snow, then took an aerial photograph of these "desire lines" to build permanent walkways, "an example of perfect planning of public space." This is this other kind of work that we are reading the fruits of, Heike Geissler's book, Katy Derbyshire's translation, this work of failure, of exhaustion, of precarity, of alienation, of splitting selves, of the labor of thought, of a romance with books, where I writes back to the absurd and homogenous lists of books You once had to catalog. The ambivalent tone of the hoard, veering from inside to outside, from shame to greed, from intimacy to alienation, is a dream of public space. So we follow the desire lines.

V

AVIARY, OR ANIMAL

OUR INVESTIGATION into tone continues, when we can find silence to think, to the sound of the constant air-conditioning, and somehow through the drone, the chirping of sparrows, as we sit on the couch not facing the windows to the outside world. We think to the history of an aviary as an enclosure, but structured to make the fence appear invisible, as well as the boundaries between the exterior and interior, the built and the natural world. This returns us to the poor demented quail that the unnamed Sebald narrator encounters at the abandoned manor at Somerleyton in *The Rings of Saturn*—back and forth, back and forth, unable to escape its cage. Whenever we read this section and consider the grainy black-and-white photograph, we wonder whether the narrator really sees and considers this creature, the nature of its solitude and captivity, an anxiety or melancholy we might call ecological, or whether the bird is an object for his projections, his despair and alienation.

We would like to posit this question into the open air—can a novel be an aviary? In Hiroko Oyamada's *The Factory*, the hermetic bryologist Yoshio Furufue begins to observe the crowded patterns of the black birds that surround the river near campus, noticing how they stare back at the human. The temporary worker Yoshiko Ushiyama, whose narration opens the novel, observes in the first line the odor of these birds that also fascinate her—later, on her mandated half day off, she will attempt to go to the bridge to see the mysterious birds, where she meets Furufue, who is taking photographs of them in order to investigate, his scientific curiosity piqued by a schoolchild visiting the factory who hands him a report on the neighboring animals, who observes that these shags are all adults, never nest, and survive on local waste. At the end of the novel, a blurry metamorphosis of all three narrators takes place—from the human to the nonhuman, with Yoshiko Ushiyama becoming one of the birds, standing by the copier, automatically feeding paper to the shredder, a return to odor as primary, to the point of view of the creaturely, to the smell of the ocean. Perhaps it's fanciful of us to imagine the photographs taken of the flocks of ominous black birds with the *are-bure-boke* quality of Japanese photobooks, the grain, blur, and mournful dark tones of Masahisa Fukase's *Ravens*, the impressionistic photographs he took in the 1970s and 1980s following a divorce, set against the coastal landscape of Hokkaido. In these speculative Japanese narratives, it is the bird or other creature who serves as a metaphor or extension for trauma and alienation. We think of a letter that Kafka wrote Felice, which has been read as an interpretation for his animal stories: "Often—and in my inmost self perhaps all the time—I doubt whether I am a human being." Yet, our Committee to Investigate Atmosphere wonders, what would a literature look like that decenters the human as sovereign, as center of the narrative? Perhaps even away from the anthropomorphic idea of voice? We have already considered, in part, the ventriloquism of Sebald's narrators. But now we think as well of how Thalia Field's "Hi Adam!" in *Personhood* performs a theater of confinement in an abandoned parrot "sanctuary" that is more chaotic prison environment, performs silence, trauma, as well as their mirroring of one another, their mimicry, how they've learned to speak the language of their captors. With tone we also think of atonal, of the screeching or irritation of captive parrots parroting one another. With tone we think of the ensemble tone, after Fred Moten. This will guide our investigation into the aviary, or the animal, as it relates to tone and the collective. Deleuze and Guattari write that one of the values of minor literature is that everything is collective: the individual utterance becomes the collective utterance. In Kafka's animal stories, such as "Josephine the Singer, or the Mouse Folk" and "Investigations of a Dog," they write, "There is no subject: *there are only collective arrangements of utterance*." Perhaps the originary investigations into atmosphere, the speaker of each of these stories, if we can individuate the first person plural of the Josephine story as a speaker, investigates the subject's dissolution into tone, wondering about their role as an individual in a community. "But is not everybody silent exactly in the same way?"

As we consider our investigation into the "ensemble of the senses" being the "ensemble of the social," the committee would like to submit a found report, *The Guideline on Odor in Ambient Air*, used for odor regulation in Germany. Field investigations by the authority, which measure the annual odor frequency, found a correlation between odor intensity and odor annoyance. In further field measurements, odor intensity was linked to hedonic tone, the capacity to experience pleasure (as compared to low hedonic tone, which increases the likelihood of anhedonia). The hedonic tone of air pollution depends on the character of the odor and how annoying it is. We wonder what this means in terms of our inquiry into an "atmospheric commons," as located within the fictions we are studying. Others are irritating if they give off an odor, of food, smoke, sweat, the animal, if they are crowded together in an interior (a train, a cubicle, an apartment, a factory, an aviary). How strange that the opening of *The Factory*—Yoshiko Ushiyama smelling the odor of birds in the office where she is being interviewed—shares an atmosphere with the opening of Mieko Kanai's 1972 "Rabbits," a story we have been reading and rereading, together and alone, for decades. Both narrators experience anhedonia in their waking lives and find themselves awakened to a maze-like atmosphere (whether going down a rabbit hole or trying to navigate the hierarchies of a mysterious corporation), which leads them closer to the other, the creaturely, which is characterized by an intense odor. It is this anhedonia at the beginning of "Rabbits" that makes the narrator feel followed by "an odor like that of an unseen bird that had flown right past my nose." There's something ineffable about the odor, the narrator goes on to think, or, if not an odor, something that takes on the form of an odor, like an illusion, something ephemeral and elusive that disappears. The description of this mysterious smell continues, a smell that comes from "deep within me" and is accompanied by nausea. Note the confusion of the inside and outside that characterizes a tone as that of the collective or ensemble. We are reminded of Fred Moten's line that "the solo is an emanation of the ensemble." An emanation suggests the ghostly or uncanny—what is emitted or radiated; it can be gas or odor or light or sound. We sense the humanimal character Lily, who throughout the story transforms by her own volition and desire into a rabbit, before we can smell her, sense her from within the writer-narrator, who is perhaps inventing her or has already internalized her. Perhaps we can characterize these Japanese novels as within a creaturely, even glandular literature.

A glandular literature would have, we surmise, a particularly intense relationship to the body. Could tone be a pheromonal signal? We remember teaching Mieko Kanai's "Rabbits," and how a student protested that she found the story so disgusting she could not reread it to prepare for the final exam. The story, which we scanned from Phyllis Birnbaum's translated volume and distributed in the presumably odorless form of a PDF file, seems haunted by what the narrator describes as a "strange animal smell," a "vile" odor that "made my stomach turn over." It's the smell of fur and blood, of the rabbits Lily slaughters, like her father before her, a smell that eventually drives the rest of the family from the house, leaving the father and daughter in a sanguinary idyll suffused with what Lily remembers fondly as her father's "warm animal smell." Lily's joy, the pleasure she takes in raising and killing rabbits, produces a discordant tone, something like a constant alarming noise. One theory of the etymology of "noise" relates it to nausea, and we wonder if it is less Lily's actions that repel some readers than the dissonance of her persistent and inexplicable happiness. She bathes in rabbit gore, neatly arranging her blood-soaked pubic hair. She hops around in a costume of rotting rabbit skins. When her father, terrified, throws a pitcher at her (the violent use of a household object recalling Gregor Samsa's father attacking him with the nourishing, domestic apples), the broken glass of her pink rabbit eyepiece lodges in her eye, and she finds her ravaged face "startlingly pretty." We remember Gilles Deleuze's emphasis, in his description of what he calls becoming-animal, on a specific project: "*to dismantle the face.*" "Now I am completely a rabbit," says Lily. But she is not a rabbit; she is, and remains throughout the story, a transitional creature. She exists in what Deleuze and Guattari, in *Kafka: Toward a Minor Literature*, call "a world of pure intensities where all forms come undone." A world whose odor nauseates, whose noise does not resolve. The intensity of this in-between place reminds us that the word "horror," which in the early fourteenth century meant "a feeling of disgust," perhaps similar to nausea, derives from the Latin noun meaning "dread, veneration, religious awe," which comes from the verb *horrere*, to shudder or bristle with fear. Horror raises the hair. It's related to the Latin word for hedgehog. It marks an experience humans share with certain other animals: a prickling sensation, a ruffling of the feathers. For our student, as for ourselves, "Rabbits" gets under the skin, provoking a direct physical response. We recall the observation of A. E. Housman: "Experience has taught me, when I am shaving of a morning, to keep watch over my thoughts, because, if a line of poetry strays into my memory, my skin bristles so that the razor ceases to act."

As we consider the blade of the razor against prickly animal skin, while remembering the Sebald narrator's photographic encounter with the quail, we want to explore how tone involves the nonhuman, how the aviary's atmosphere is both bird and cage, infusing them, surrounding them, constituted by them, affecting them. The preposition *between* suggests the arrangement that produces this tone: between fence and feather, between camera and creature. We recall the transformation at the conclusion of *The Factory*, which is both animal and technological. It's based on an experience Oyamada had as a temporary worker at a car factory, which she describes in an interview:

> I looked up and saw a woman by one of the printers, holding a giant black bird by its wings. . . . When I took another look, it wasn't a bird at all. It was a part for the printer— maybe a toner cartridge. Still, the image of that bird in the basement stuck with me. . . . In that moment, I found what I needed to finish the novella. A little while after that, I quit my job at the factory.

The nonexistent bird seen by mistake in the real-world factory becomes a genuine bird in the fantasy factory, a bird into which Yoshiko slips, as if into the blackness of ink, through it and out of it. This marks the moment of quitting, the end of the text.

When the aviary opens, does writing end? In "Rabbits," somatic intensities overwhelm and replace language: the narrator, having returned to the house to find Lily dead, puts on the dead girl's rabbit fur and crouches among the rabbits, remaining "in that same spot, absolutely still." This narrator, who began the story by declaring that writing is her fate, seems to have arrived at the end of writing, just as, in *The Factory*, Yoshiko's transformation into a bird brings the novel to an abrupt close. Are these texts portraying the writing of the animal as impossible? Or can the openness of a spreading wing infuse a text with an altered shade, the ink wash suggested by the image of a toner cartridge? We recall the space and silence at the heart of Ibrahim al-Koni's *The Bleeding of the Stone*, a novel whose protagonist, Asouf, a reclusive herdsman in the Libyan desert, transforms into a wild sheep to escape conscription into the colonial army. The novel undergoes a shift in perspective at that moment, a transformation in tone we think of, once again, as spatial, dependent on a particular arrangement of things, in this case the relationship between Asouf and the narrative voice. Up to this point in the novel, the reader has followed Asouf through close third-person narration, with direct access to his experience. But suddenly there's a gap. Asouf's thoughts and feelings fade away. We see him from a distance, among the other conscripts, "packed together like sheep"—an image that marks the structural kinship between the colonized and the animal, the extinction threatening both the wild sheep and the nomadic lifeways of Asouf, whose name is the Tamasheq word for "wild space." Then even his body disappears, and we learn of him only through hearsay, through the legends of the people of the oasis, the young men who claim they've seen a miracle, a man changing into a wild sheep and bounding up the mountainside, escaping the Italians' bullets. Just as suddenly as he vanished, Asouf appears again, human now, tending his camels. He will never refer to his transformation. He will never recall it for the reader, never confirm how he escaped the army. His moment of becoming-animal is a silence. Or perhaps, instead of a silence, it would be more accurate to call it an ensemble sound, for this experience seems to require a collective narration, both human and nonhuman, composed of the young men of the oasis, the Sufis who declare Asouf a saint, the wind-like whoosh of the sheep up the rocks, even the crack of bullets. As if the individual voice of the narrator transmitting Asouf's thoughts is insufficient for the task at hand. Asouf dissolves into the wild space he both inhabits and embodies, into the echo of the Sufis praising God all night, reminding us of the meditation on collective sound in Ted Chiang's story "The Great Silence." This story was written in collaboration with the artists Jennifer Allora and Guillermo Calzadilla, part of a video installation, both animal and technological, that collages the Arecibo telescope in Puerto Rico with the endangered parrots in the surrounding forest. "The Great Silence" references the Fermi paradox, which asks why humans have never found an alien intelligence in the vast universe. Narrated by a parrot, Chiang's story proposes that the aliens we seek are already here: they are animals, whom we may drive to extinction before we can hear them. The parrot-narrator, a lover of sound, expresses an affinity for the chanting of the Pythagorean mystics, Pentecostal speaking in tongues, and Hindu mantras. The Arecibo telescope, the parrot tells us, picks up a faint hum between the stars. A residue of the Big Bang, it is the sound of creation.

One of the young daughters of the committee is currently in the stage of liking to draw animals but not feeling confident as to whether she can draw animals in a realistic way. We tell her that it can be blurred, this drawing of the animal. What is the feeling inside the animal, the feeling of the animal? we ask her. Writing this, we think inside the animal, of the feeling of the animal, of the transformation of a narrative voice that we explored in the previous paragraph, a transformation in tone that is spatial. The committee would like to call attention to a 2013 video on YouTube in which the philosopher Donna Haraway is asked to define the term "humanimal." Haraway uses a gestural language in order to define this concept spatially. She displays her fists side by side and tells us it's a hybrid term that puts human and animal together. The sides of her fists repeatedly bang together. "And makes them come inside each other." The fingers interlock then dance around one another. Haraway goes on to say that she thinks of it as "a linguistic way of paying attention to the way that humans and animals co-make each other in the making of history." It is, she says, useful for our purposes here, a way of thinking that is multiple as well as symbiotic. You can't, she says, think of these species one at a time but must think among these species and between species, in understanding the world as it is now, in terms of our relations of labor and cruelty and care.

In trying to imagine the possibilities of writing the animal, and perhaps within this, paying attention to the boundary between animal and human, the committee looks with curiosity to Clarice Lispector's "The Buffalo," translated by Katrina Dodson, a potential example of "zoopoetics," the term Derrida coined to describe Kafka's animal stories. What a strange beast of a story this is, all body and blurred consciousness. The story is written in a third-person interior, a defamiliarized point of view, where the lines between the interior and the exterior dissolve, much like, briefly, the bars of the zoo the woman is visiting, desiring to become undone, to be outside of herself in the intensities of erotic hatred, an abjection to this desired alterity. Can we briefly circle back to the kindred "Rabbits," the metamorphosis depicted as the interior dissolving into the exterior? The animal "pervading the interior" in the form of this strong odor? The house becoming a hutch or burrow? This internalized external space is perhaps inspired by Kafka's own unfinished "The Burrow," a hibernating rodent of some indiscernible (blurry) type who speaks of his home as if it's both inside and outside. The paranoid creature is the burrow and also must stand vigil over it, to ensure the secure perimeter is not violated; the burrow is the only being he can trust. There is no inside or outside of the burrow, its careful arrangement of hoarded rooms.

Deleuze and Guattari, writing as a collective, in "Becoming-Intense, Becoming-Animal, Becoming-Imperceptible," write that "becoming" and "multiplicity" feed each other, like Donna Haraway's fingers linked together, a forming and unforming into the others. "Thus packs, or multiplicities, continually transform themselves into each other, crossing over into each other." In Mieko Kanai's "Rabbits," in order for Lily to become-rabbit, she intentionally blinds herself, the narrator also huddled silent and still at the end with the colony. In "The Buffalo," there is no real reciprocity between the woman and the zoo animals, her gaze annihilating the series of animals in cages into herself. "Her eyes were so focused on searching that her vision sometimes darkened into a kind of sleep, and then she'd recompose herself as if in the coolness of a pit." In Lispector's story, the unnamed woman desires to animalize herself, which is experienced through a mute yet emotional intensity (the becoming-animal perhaps a way for silence to be rendered in tone in a textual space). If her searching to become animal is rendered in silence, it is possibly also an ensemble silence, the caged animals who stare back still without words (the lions, the giraffe "more landscape than being," the birds, the naked monkey, the hippo, the chewing camel, the coati, finally the black blot of the buffalo). The ensemble sound is the woman's moan echoing back at herself, the sound of her body merging with the animal and landscape, amid the sky and the buffalo, in the final act of syncope (the humanimal comes together). The only scream is on the roller coaster, where she is also merged with other humans, but she forgets to use this collective body to let out her own howl.

Yet is the animal even present in Lispector's story, except as fantasy and projection? In "Why Look at Animals?" John Berger writes that it is impossible to really see animals in the zoo, because "the view is always wrong." The zoo, after Berger, is a monument to the animal's disappearance, a spectacle of industrial capitalism that shows the rupture of intimacy that still exists between animals and humans in rural and small agricultural societies and the role of animals as "messengers and promises." With humans, Berger notes, the abyss can be bridged by language, but with human and animal, the abyss is that of nonreciprocity or nonrecognition. Derrida likewise writes that we have constructed animals in our own language, in our own reflection. The animal looking at us is always the other. Haraway, critiquing Derrida, suggests that "we polish an animal mirror to look for ourselves." We can ask ourselves, rephrasing Haraway with a question, what would it mean for a literary work to look back at animals, more than depicting animals looking at us? How is it possible to approach the animal in a spirit of listening? As an experiment in conversation? We are thinking of Robin Wall Kimmerer's experiments in listening in *Braiding Sweetgrass* that acknowledge reciprocity among species in indigenous ways of knowledge, that think through labor and care of the herd of buffalo grazing on grass, that allow grass to grow faster.

Perhaps the answer also lies in the tone of the ensemble, which can be the blurred language of the humanimal that veers from silence into "an embodied, multiply-voiced utterance," such as in Bhanu Kapil's *Humanimal*, a first-person hybrid narrative that partially tells the story of and through Amala and Kamala, the mysterious Bengali "wolf-girls" and feral children allegedly extracted from a wolf den by the Christian missionary

Reverend J. A. L. Singh, as he documents in his diary, who along with his wife attempts to "reeducate" them both by language lessons, moral lessons, and a regime of painful massage and physical training to walk upright. *Humanimal* is written in blocks of text that collage voices and echoes of animality, colonialism, and violence—the voice of Kamala, who tragically survives her sister and learns limited language to care for the other young charges at the orphanage, as well as Kapil's father and Kapil's own origins of outsiderness and experiences of racism, being treated as animal.

Walking into town, we gaze through a rusted fence at a sign: *All Animals Must Be Registered.* But there are no animals here, only empty, bunker-like sheds. The sign has been shoved behind one of these structures, crooked, maybe discarded. We consider the resonance of the phrase *to register the animal.* To enroll, to indicate, to note, to perceive. At the restaurant we read *Humanimal,* this text of transitory and feral creatures, of Amala and Kamala forced toward the human, Amala almost immediately dying of it, her sister imagined by Kapil in an ongoing hybrid space. Kamala is moving from wolf to girl, while the characters in "Rabbits" and "The Buffalo" are moving the other way, from the human toward the animal; all of them inhabit an interspecies contact zone where gesture is both a signal and a mystery. In "Rabbits," Lily's gestures seem calculated to provoke horror and disgust in humans, the way they do in her father, but this interpretation fails, for Lily wished only to please him. Her pleasure can't communicate itself to humans, it's deviant, it deviates, it gets lost. We consider the humanimal tone, intensely gestural and enigmatic, simultaneously momentous and remote, a language of pressure and moan, of tightening, turning, scratching, and chewing, with an insistent erotic charge. We remember the woman in "The Buffalo" shaking the fence around the buffalo's paddock while a "white thing was spreading inside her, viscous like a kind of saliva." The image of saliva so intimate, the white thing utterly unknown, it might be something from another world, the white streak of a distant galaxy. We hypothesize that the humanimal tone joins the visceral to the abstract. We are eating a salad and drinking green tea. Everything tastes like leaves. We consider the powerful attachments conveyed by our glandular texts, these sizzling, uneven connections, with a fraught quality we might call frayed, the interspecies entanglements that reject the smooth registration and production processes of corporate space, creating instead a rough, stinging effect like that of hair catching when different skins touch. In *Humanimal* we read, "the girl reached up, her arms criss-crossing rapidly." We sniff the book cautiously, checking for any lingering odor to the slightly stiff, rippled pages, which our cat peed on in 2014. We think it smells fine. We think it's all right to read this book at the table. We read, "Reaching and touching were the beginning actions."

We are fortified by the links Kapil draws between animals, girls, colonized people, and children, her acknowledgment of this matrix of disempowerment, which Sylvia Wynter calls the archipelago of Human Otherness. For the stakes of becoming-animal differ depending on one's human body. Dismantling the face will have a particular resonance for one who is already said to have little face. In a reading of Deleuze and Guattari, Gerald L. Bruns remarks: "The white European male face defines the apex from which humanity declines by degrees into the faces of women, children, non-Westerners, subalterns, aborigines, hominids, troglodytes, chimpanzees, pets, bats, flies." Kapil holds this thick mess of human cultural material clustered over the animal, the sticky and fertile stuff of the co-making process, like the "vernix or matte" clumped on the bodies and hair of Amala and Kamala, an in-between matter that once connected them to their wolf siblings. It is from an already not-quite-human position that our chosen texts imagine the jagged and potent gestures of the humanimal zone. They are attuned to this zone, bent upon it despite the risks. They are not interested in climbing the hierarchy to reach the apex of humanity or even in expanding or recuperating the human face, this face that, Deleuze and Guattari maintain, is produced by separating the head from the body through what they term capitalism's "facial machine." If, as the Deleuze-Guattari committee writes, "the face is a politics," then our humanimal texts are allied with the project of smashing that politics, of rending and polluting and stinking up the terms of their own omission from the possibility of being cared for or even just granted some space. When shown a photograph in which her dead sister Amala has been registered, Kamala responds with three gestures: looking away, crying, ripping. "She destroyed the paper. She killed her face." When Kamala herself is photographed, she howls at a passing bird so that the resulting image is blurry. "Two faces blossom from one thin neck." She blurs and multiplies herself, as if to return to the litter of cubs, to the company of her lost sister.

Killing the face is the way to enter the pack. At the next table, a family arrives, two adults, two small children, and a newborn baby. We note the father's T-shirt with a picture of a horned bull like the black, almost featureless face of Lispector's buffalo. The children are fussing. A kind lady nearby tries to distract them with talk, telling them they must read a book called *The Elephant and the Ant*. She wants to know if they've read the Berenstain Bears. We consider the link between children and animals, this psychosocial humanimal glue, eventually outgrown like vernix. The children clamor to see the bear. They want to visit the bear who lives in the hallway between the restaurant and the visitors' center, a model taller than they are, fascinating, rigid. This bear is made of painted wood or plastic. We've never touched it. It wears an advertisement for a statuary garden around its neck. A sad gaze over its shoulder toward the door. The children creep toward it, excited, hand in hand, still becoming human. We return to Bhanu Kapil's "project for future children," this text she terms a "blue sky fiction," observing the floating patches of color that mark our animal texts, as thickly present as gestures. *The Factory*: "I saw gray, and a little green." Rough, smeared, and out of focus. We remember Alex, the African gray parrot described in "The Great Silence," who could understand the concepts of shape and color. *Humanimal*: "Blue as blue then brown then green then black."

We remember such a bear statue outside wood-paneled restaurants on road trips as children. Now it blurs in our mind with the bear who promoted fire safety. We look to the sky colored with scrawled blue crayon, punctuated by the darker *V*'s of birds, and wonder as a committee how to further investigate atmosphere in these "animal stories," as Kafka called his parables. While waiting for the smoke to clear, we remember the photograph in the newspaper, taken at the conference on climate change in Glasgow, of the display of identical polar bear statues wearing life vests, at the pavilion of the endangered archipelago of Tuvalu. It's a metaphor, said Vincent J. F. Huang, the Taiwanese artist who created the statues, to get media attention for the rising sea levels of the Polynesian island people who themselves emit little CO_2. The hope is also that the myriads taking selfies in front of the polar bears will experience an ecological feeling, a sudden awareness of an atmospheric commons. Isn't that partially the reason for all of these animal stories for children, the parade of miniatures, the books? The mechanical growl of the polar bear when you press the button. But does the Sebald narrator actually encounter the taxidermied polar bear at the dilapidated manor in *The Rings of Saturn*, imagining the bear navigating his hundred-mile treks to find food? The question is not only whether polar bears exist to human beings but whether human beings exist to polar bears. In our investigation we think of Barry Lopez's decision to stop photographing polar bears in his pilgrimages in the Arctic, when he encountered a young male bear in September 1981 and realized that with his compulsion to shoot him with a camera he was violating the animal's space, refusing the desired distance:

> I got back to the ship and lay down on my bunk and realized that I had entirely missed the bear. Then I forced myself

to remember every move the bear had made, whether his head turned left or right, how far he swam, how long he hesitated before he got up on a piece of ice. I decided that photographing that polar bear was a sort of pinup approach to nature. I decided never again to let the camera come between me, the animal and the landscape.

Our mind wanders to Yoko Tawada's triptych of three little bears, *Memoirs of a Polar Bear,* translated into the German by the author and then translated into the English by Susan Bernofsky, where she writes three matrilineal generations of the polar bear as alienated worker, first as an exiled writer, then as exploited circus performer, and finally as the global phenomenon of Knut at the Berlin Zoo, rejected by his mother, Tosca, alienated as a tabloid celebrity from his own image and narrative. Like the uncanny multiplicity of grinning polar bears at the UN conference, Knut became a symbol, of a present we can't know and a future we can't imagine, a way for a mass audience to confront climate change but also, crucially and cynically, a moneymaker for the Berlin Zoo, in the form of ticket sales. Tawada deconstructs how we entirely miss the bear, the multiplicity of Baby Knut's image and self into key chains, stuffed animals, and photographs, the crowd projecting a happiness onto the captive and cuddly-looking bear. Reminiscent of the second part of the novel, from the point of view of Tosca's handler for the German National Circus, that illuminates the blurriness of the humanimal bond, of the surrogate mothers within the systems of captivity, we are reminded of a quote from the animal trainer Doris Arndt in her obituary, the black-and-white photograph of her posed with a pyramid of polar bears behind her, when she refuted Knut's trainer that the cub had smiled at him. "Polar bears don't make faces; they have only three black points, whether they are playing or they are angry," she had told a Berlin newspaper at the time. Tawada depicts a porous and atmospheric interiority for the bear's life in captivity, how time moves in a layered way, a primal sense of ancestral history, Knut only able to commune with the ghost of Michael Jackson as well as the premonition of his unknown mother and grandmother, confused about who the "I" is and who is "Knut," clutching his stuffed animal self at night. Although polar bears in the wild are solitary creatures, spending much of their lives wandering immense distances by themselves, except for the early years the mother bear spends with her cubs, Tawada depicts the existential state of the captive polar bear as emotionally dependent on humans, fearing abandonment, mourning for an open landscape they never remembered encountering, and alienated from their essential being. "Time was a huge ice block made of loneliness." The entire affective existence of Knut is depicted as encountering the outside world and other beings (the humans and the animals) entirely through tone. "Whenever Matias left the room, the bear metamorphosed into a listening ear." In this last part of Tawada's novel, as in our other animal stories, ensemble tone is imagined in colors. "The heard world was so commodious, so rich in colors." When I/Knut listens to the aviary, a flamingo's sentence is pink.

VI

GUEST LECTURE, OR REPORTS
TO AN ACADEMY

AT THE conference, a few minutes before the panel begins, the Committee to Investigate Atmosphere moves through a hall. We search for the restroom. We have walked a long way, and our feet are beginning to cramp. At last we sit at a table against a wall and are told to speak into the Owl, a black box that will transmit our voices and images to a virtual audience. The Owl has lighted circles in it like eyes. We angle our bodies to appear in its line of sight, thinking of the grandmother polar bear in Tawada's novel, a writer well accustomed to literary conferences, who informs us, "Every conference is a circus." The polar bear recalls being taught, through a combination of pleasure and pain, of lashings and sugar, to stand on her hind legs in a circus ring. Now she is also thoroughly trained in the performative art of the conference, shooting her paw into the air in order to request to speak, proud of her speed until she notices it's just a reflex. She must have been enticed and punished in order to develop this marvelously quick reaction to the conference panel. "I felt this realization," she declares, "like a stab in the chest." The committee would like to investigate the tone of the talking animal, the alien or guest speaker who articulates with care into the vaguely threatening space of the lecture hall. We are struck by the high incidence, among our atmospheric samples, of the meeting of animals and scholarly diction, from Kafka's "Report to an Academy" to the treatise on animals in *The Factory* to Ted Chiang's erudite parrot, a connection that evokes the animal's role as a research subject and seems to include the humanimal elements of the visceral and the abstract, but arranged in a way that, rather than building toward violence, as in "Rabbits" or "The Buffalo," is playful and wistful, moving toward the parodic or carnivalesque. These creatures are so well behaved, so tame. Only certain gestures still indicate their awkwardness, the impossibility of belonging, the literary bear charmed by the rhythm of her own language into dancing in her seat so that the chair creaks beneath her. Her unseemliness filters through the abstract language and formal codes of the conference panel. Her gestures reveal the visceral impact of training, of the education required in order to attend the conference at all, to shape the kind of words we are saying now, as we slip our shoes off under the table.

We smile nervously as the tenured head of the Department of Narrative introduces us, looking down at our notes, sometimes glancing at each other, wondering if the Owl is sensitive enough to pick up the awkwardness of our body language. The introductions are made with a certain gesture of the hand at us and a few chords of language reading our qualifications. But we would like more time to collect ourselves; we are unsure who we are, here, at this elite university in which each of us is a guest, one of us taking the train in from another state, the other the curious designation of semipermanent guest, celebrated in the moment yet perpetually temporary. We are unsure what the particular dance we are expected to perform is. It is a duet, we know. It is our turn to turn on. We begin reading from our notes, which are as usual letters to each other, which almost feel too intimate to speak out loud in this cramped conference room, too much a private language. The panel speaks with one body. Our table a barrier between us and the audience, whom we hope are smiling at us through their masks; we try to make eye contact, making everyone feel special. When it is our turn, we look at the lecture notes and speak of sharing space with each other, which we think is speaking of narrative. Even though we are *in person*, as they now say, we go into these other spaces when we speak, the other spaces we have shared. Afterward, for the Q&A, we have to echo the questions of others back to the Owl. They want to know about the life of the writer. We want to be of service. The time we are allotted is partial, so fragments fall out. Our mouths repeatedly make the shape of the word *epistolary* until we're not sure what it means. We are not confident, like the hybrid we are speaking into, that we will get smarter over time. We feel like the speaker in one of Renee Gladman's *Calamities*, returning to the uneasy site of the classroom or lecture hall, trying through gestures to enact community as a feeling, to articulate abstracted theories of narrative. These lecture performances in *Calamities* are of the awkward impasse of language, of how to think together, speaking in front of the classroom, later listening in an audience. Maybe it's only correct that these communications read elliptically, bridging silences by miming language, with emphatic nods and facial expressions. "I said, '—' and made a certain gesture with my hand." How unreal and draining it all is, this meeting place, that we are allowed to have naked faces that grimace and laugh and smile too hard, in order for us to communicate good feelings to the audience in front of us, who have disappeared from view, and the other hidden audience as well, who sees us, we realize later, in a fish-eyed view that includes all persons equally and facilitates natural collaboration, the technology promises. There is a buzzing sensation in the air we can't quite track. We realize we have now moved together past realism into something more speculative. The speaker is up there alone. It is a lonely feeling, the lecture tone. We always want to bring up Kafka's animal stories, especially when no one wants us to bring up Kafka; perhaps it's why we long to, our shared perversity. The subject compelled to speak, to prove that they are human. How lonely they seem. "The lecture hall may be nothing but a zoo." How long since we have spoken to each other about the lectures of Elizabeth Costello as a secret language. We have regarded them as curious, even ambivalent, objects, these series of fictionalized lectures through the alter ego of J. M. Coetzee, who chooses to discourse on the suffering and lives of animals, based on his own appearances, as opposed to what Elizabeth Costello is expected to discourse on, assumedly feminist literature, as she is most famously the author of a novel from the point of view of Molly Bloom. But in reality no one, we think, expects

Coetzee to lecture on anything in minor tones; everything is major, because it's coming from his mouth. In the first story, "Realism," Elizabeth Costello is traveling to Pennsylvania with her son, John, a physics professor who serves as the third-person narrator, to receive a major literary prize and award. She is later told through murmurings that she is the Australian candidate for the prize, the woman candidate, when she wishes to be just the candidate. Throughout, the extractive labor of traveling and performing is shown—the facts of an aging body, which becomes worn out from interviews, overcome with jetlag. Her son, her minder, through whose narrative gaze we see the aging author, thinks his mother reminds him of a tired old circus seal. She herself identifies with Red Peter and performs in her met-alecture a close reading of Kafka's monologue of a lecturing ape who has learned to speak his audience's language and mastered their manners in order to survive. Unlike the narrative we are reading, we note Costello's observation, in her reading of "A Report to an Academy," that the form of a lecture doesn't involve that the speaker or audience be investigated by the narrative gaze. We know that the Owl/Audience is watching us, but they are not on screen. The question in "Realism" is that of tone, we realize. Not only the hybridity of who is speaking—both the narrator John in a third-person realistic story and also Elizabeth Costello in the lecture form—but also who is allowed, in fiction, to occupy other tones. This is also a meta-question—can Coetzee adopt a woman's point of view? Did Kafka actually occupy the tone of an ape, or did the ape occupy the tone of a human? Perhaps, Elizabeth Costello speculates, half seriously, the story is actually parrots speaking to parrots. A radio journalist who has a brief affair with Elizabeth Costello's son, her ambassador in the story of her position, critiques the famed writer when she attempts to write from other positions, meaning men or dogs. Mimicry, she says. What the audience wants is for her to speak from her natural tone, the tone of being a woman. That is the collectivity she is expected to speak from and to, when commissioned to speak before an audience. An uneasy feeling reading *Elizabeth Costello*—to see a familiar grievance multiplied into other voices. We wonder again if this blurriness can be described as tonal.

We think of Helga Crane, with her avian surname, dressed in her garish clothes in Denmark, under pressure to perform something naturally colorful, simple, and sultry. What a disappointment it would have been for her audience if she had begun talking about Kafka! But Kafka, with his sad and cheerful story of Red Peter, captures the absurdity of the demands placed on Helga Crane, the insistence on the performance of the natural, the dizzying blend of mimicry, training, and desire that makes us so anxious to do a good job for the Owl, to give something of ourselves. To give what, exactly? "The first thing I learned was to give a handshake," Red Peter reports; "a handshake betokens frankness." Honored members of the Academy! We would like to be entirely frank with you, but the lecture room prevents us, the chairs are too hard, you're too far away, some of you are invisible, and this table is hitting us right between the ribs. The tone of the guest lecture is conditioned by being *in front of*: a prepositional arrangement of distance and exposure. But we would like you to come outside with us, to the large, strange, empty tent where, before this panel began, we sat eating peanuts and raisins from a napkin. Wires crossed the ground beneath this tent and supported the bulbs that hung above us, unlighted in the bright spring afternoon. Some performance or celebration had taken place in this tent or would be starting later, but for the time being nobody else was there, and the curious indoor-outdoor space, with its pleasant shadows, seemed devoted to a single purpose, which was that we should drink our coffees and gobble those snacks before we went onstage. All universities possess such temporarily or permanently disused spaces. Students find them. Sometimes they are occupied by that shifting collective Harney and Moten term the undercommons, the graduate students and adjuncts and other workers of dubious status who undertake forms of study the classroom renders impossible. We remember reading *The Undercommons* during our first year of teaching, how forcibly we were struck by the interview at the end, by Fred Moten's question about university work and feeling:

> We were trying to understand this problematic of our own alienation from our capacity to study—the exploitation of our capacity to study that was manifest as a set of academic products. That's what we were trying to understand. And it struck us that this is what workers who are also thinkers have always been trying to understand. How come we can't be together and think together in a way that feels good, the way it should feel good? For most of our colleagues and students, however much you want to blur that distinction, that question is the hardest question to get people to consider. . . .

There are lots of people who are angry and who don't feel good, but it seems hard for people to ask, collectively, "why doesn't this feel good?"

When we read this, we felt good. It was as if we had entered the space of the undercommons, as if Harney and Moten had opened a door for us, as if there was a tent inside the text, something impermanent and flimsy but for that very reason mobile, light, and easy to repurpose. It was something we could use. We felt that it had been built for us. And this is the same feeling we have when reading Kafka and Tawada, these performing animal texts that affirm, with a muffled growl of laughter, that when somebody puts a hot pipe against your fur, it doesn't feel good. Oh, certainly, one takes it; one gets over the stage Red Peter describes, when he screams internally, "To get out somewhere, to get out! Only not to stay motionless with raised arms, crushed against a wooden wall." Eventually, one learns how to perform, how to drink schnapps and write academic reports. But an obscure energy remains, like the question "why doesn't this feel good?"—the dark residue of one's capacity to study. We think of the German title of *Memoirs of a Polar Bear*: *Etüden im Schnee*, which we have seen glossed as "Études in the Snow," "Studies in the Snow," and "Musical Exercises in the Snow." And the title of the earlier Japanese "partner text" as well: *Yuki no renshūsei*, "The Trainee of Snow" or "The Snow Apprentice." This is a book of study. It has an undercommon tone, an air of exile and unsuccessful training, of poorly executed, jangling notes whose failure and awkwardness incarnate the desire for a different method. Flash of memory: Yoko Tawada at a conference, years ago. We sat in the audience. We no longer recall what Tawada said or even what language she spoke, whether she spoke English or whether someone translated for her, but we do remember that the conversation turned to the language of Kafka. And someone—Tawada? another panelist?—said that Kafka's language was neither standard German nor Prague German nor German inflected with Yiddish, that it was an alien German, unrelated to anything before or since, a form of expression that struck the earth like a meteorite. What feels good about the undercommon tone, what gives us a feeling of kinship, as if these texts are building a secret workshop with us, is precisely the discomfiting, extraterrestrial form of the guest lecture, the outsider quality of *guest* and the formality of *lecture* combining to preclude the possibility of anything unlabored, the awkward position *in front of* announcing hey, excuse us, honored members of the Academy, there is nothing natural to be extracted from this conference, because we are a bunch of apprentices, and the only tone available to us is the one used by half-trained apes and half-employed polar bears, by visiting immigrant creatures, self-translating performing writers, furry circus riders who are asked to define their ethnicity at the border, native speakers of asteroid dialects, and men who are women who talk about Kafka. To be frank: an impostor tone.

Where are we as we're writing this? We are feeling somewhat dizzy, so we are lying down. We have been refreshing our email all day, waiting with dread for the editor of our manuscript of partially autobiographical essays—no, let's call it a memoir, for commercial reasons—to get back to us with pro-posed revisions, even though it is a holiday weekend, we are still expected to work, without stopping, whenever we get the call. We must always be available. We cannot say no, or perhaps no one will print our autobiographies, which are not really autobi-ographies. To soothe ourselves with these bad publishing feel-ings, which is a doubling feeling of the undercommons, we open our copy of *Memoirs of a Polar Bear* to read the guest tone, the impostor tone, always afraid of being told we cannot exist any longer. The grandmother polar bear is precarious in her current status as retired former circus star, and as a result of this she finds herself saying yes to all manner of "service," as they say, organizing and running these perpetual conferences, the bureaucracy of this circuit, looking after the official guests of the circus, the business luncheons, the formal receptions. At least at these functions she can eat—she is starving all the time; like us she eats bird food out of baggies. The bodily feelings of the impostor tone. Always exhausted and hungry. They will feed us, but at appointed times, and they cannot tell us where the pantry is. The callous whims of "host logic," as Bhanu Kapil theorizes in her poem-essay on precarity, "How to Wash a Heart": "It's exhausting to be a guest / In somebody's house / Forever." At first we forgot to write how hungry and shaky we were, before the panel, as we stumbled through campus. We wondered at first whether to write this exhausted performance, so often omitted, only glimpsed, from a lecture tone. As Glad-man writes in *Toaf (To After That)*, the outside narrative of the essay from the inside narrative. The present-day of the grand-mother polar bear, ransacking the salmon doled out in incremental amounts in the guest fridge, ravenous from being asked to write her childhood trauma on a schedule, first from her publisher, later her translator, who smells of lies. The dread of doing something wrong paralyzes us, like we are perpetually kindergarteners. If you are told you are always not good enough, that aids in the exploitation of your labor. The spirit of passivity and refusal that is the guest tone, the guest feeling. The refusal is in the writing. It feels good to write, but to write in a diary, to write our gestures and bodies, our thoughts on writing. The diary is where to put our guest feelings, it helps document our present day. It is there we can write wrongly. The shame and desire to write in this way. The grandmother polar bear, exhausted after the conference, forces her body over to the hotel window (standing at the window is guest tone).

Where am I at this moment? I'm in my story—gone. To come back, I drag my eyes away from the manuscript and let my gaze drift toward the window until finally I'm here again, in the present. But where is *here*, when is *now*?

Why, the grandmother polar bear wonders, can't she write in the present, like Kafka's animals? The guest lecturer dreams of a right to opacity, not to be forced to write of an authentic-enough childhood. We are reminded of the moment of refusal in Bhanu Kapil's *Ban en Banlieue*, the gesture of deleting a file of childhood stories. "No, I don't think so."

And wasn't this what had first inspired our investigations? The possibility of immersing ourselves in the space of literature, unsystematically, recklessly, and together, with a merged and opaque utterance that would displace the demand for individual authenticity. The ways we had been taught to write about books would fall away: the claims to expertise, the recitation of the right names in the requisite order, the mannerly close reading, the painstakingly defended yet modest conclusion, then the writer's name and the title of her institution. Instead we would seize what we longed for: the act of reading, with all the communal energy that has always defined language and literature for us. Together we would feel our way through the fog, the dusty plains, the cramped and cluttered rooms, the zoo, the lecture hall. Today we are reading a book about writing, *Craft in the Real World* by Matthew Salesses, who points out that tone is rarely addressed in writing workshops, that in fact he has only heard it defined once, by Robert Boswell, who called it "the distance between the narrator and the character." We notice at once the emphasis on distance, which has become a key concept for our inquiry. But to restrict tone to the narrator and the character seems too narrow to us, as it does to Salesses. Using the example of a simple plot—"country boy moves to the city"—he notes the pervasive nature of tone, the way it "depends not only on how the author depicts the boy, but on how the author depicts the city, both from within the boy's perspective and . . . also outside of it." We note the fluctuant, molecular quality of tone in this description, its insider-outsider status, everywhere like air. We realize that tone is important to us because we read for it; it is more compelling to us than any other aspect of literature. We would read a book about a boy and a city not for the character, the setting, or the plot that evolves between them but for the quality of the atmosphere, and if we returned to the book, it would be in order to breathe that air again. But how seldom that air finds its way out of the book, into the other books written about it. We pick up *K.* by Roberto Calasso, his treatise on Kafka, one of the few works of criticism that imbibes the tone of its subject, a tone that radiates through Geoffrey Brock's English translation. We read: "All of Kafka's work is an exercise (in the way that Chopin's *Études* are exercises) on the many keys of foreignness." We hear the punctilious reportage of the narrator of "Josephine the Singer, or the Mouse Folk," the effort to convey, in a form that might be overheard speech or writing, the effects of a sound that might be singing, or perhaps merely the ordinary piping of mice, or perhaps merely a weak approximation of the most common mouse noises. The guest lecturer works hard in order to speak, but often with negligible results, like a visitor speaking a foreign language, straining like Josephine who expends all her strength to emit a pathetic whistle, so absorbed in her work that a cold draft could kill her. Yet, although she seems to be failing to sing—and here we would adjust the mouse narrator's account to suggest *because she seems to be failing*—something indelible and precious comes through. "This piping, which rises up where everyone else is pledged to silence, comes almost like a message from the whole people to each individual; Josephine's thin piping amidst grave decisions is almost like our people's precarious existence amidst the tumult of a hostile world." That's where we want to go: there, into the thin piping. We turn back to the opening passage of Calasso's book, which unlocks this space for us, the lonesome, chilly, ill-performed, inadequate embrace of the étude, the incomplete study.

> At the beginning there's a wooden bridge covered with snow. Thick snow. K. lifts his eyes "toward what seemed to be emptiness," *in die scheinbare Leere.* Literally: "toward the seeming emptiness." He knows there's something out in that emptiness: the Castle. He's never seen it before. He might never set foot in it.

So Calasso opens his study in snow. With the seeming emptiness of a landscape, dim as a lecture hall when one is standing on the stage, featureless as Josephine's breathy and almost inaudible sound, dry as an academic report composed by a resident alien. How often we've read those words, "the seeming emptiness"—*die scheinbare Leere.* Feeling again, in the snow, the absent presence of tone. How the syllable *schein-* reminds us inescapably of *shine.* In the barren landscape, the silent hall, the text, a sheen.

VII

LIGHTED WINDOW, OR STUDIES
IN ATMOSPHERE

LEAVING THE lecture hall, or is it a lecture room, we stumbled
down the stairs and were relieved to find ourselves outside. We
were walking with a group of people, who were leading us to
the luncheon set up for us. We found ourselves walking, as if
one body, yet one of us trailed the other. Where were we? Were
we really outside? Was this a sort of landscape? There was so
much green everywhere—almost endless green. We seemed to
be walking through an elevated plaza. Earlier, when trying to
navigate this unfamiliar part of campus to the large building
where the panel was being held, we found ourselves continually getting lost. No one was outside. Everyone was inside. We
knew we had to walk up to get there. How much was our vertigo from our guest status, or the altitude? Once inside, we
forgot to bring the papers to present to the security desk indi-
cating our correct status. We are an event! we cried. They
finally let us in. Writing this now, we think of the moment in

Renee Gladman's *Calamities* when the speaker sits on a campus, writing about landscape, thinking about who is allowed to be at the "university level," a little like Virginia Woolf's "I," who she provisionally fictionalizes as Mary Carmichael, thinking about who is allowed to be at leisure on the great open green of Oxbridge. From *Calamities*: "I began the day thinking about the university level—where it was and who was allowed to go there—and felt in my body a sense that there were a series of gates to pass through, a grand lawn, a series of gates and then an elevator to take you down into the earth." We are reminded as well of the grandmother polar bear needing to go sit on a bench outside of the conference center in order to think, of Helga Crane finding solace in the trees upon her walk through campus, of Heike Geissler's *You* trying to flaneur in the fake village of the Amazon warehouse, of all of Sebald's ex-academics desiring the pilgrimage of the open. As one body, walking as a chattering group, we wonder when we too have reached the university level. We keep passing large bronze sculptures of the kind often found in these campus landscapes—landscapes that aren't really landscapes. This one, a Henry Moore, was protested by the students as being too hideous and later moved to this elevated walkway, with the artificial greenery in large concrete planters. The bronze, *Reclining Figure*, is either monstrous or pastoral—one outstretched being, conjoined bodies against a green landscape. Isn't that a Henry Moore? We kept on asking but we weren't heard amid the talk, about our location, about the event, about the eventualities of the luncheon, which will be held outside. The luncheon was pleasant, although talking in person felt strange, after such absences of these conventionalities of the after event, after two years of speaking into lighted boxes, switching off and going to bed. Everyone was interested in speaking to us about our tone project, which surprised us. We were also hungry because, as mentioned previously, we had forgotten to eat all day. We didn't know what to say. What is tone? they asked, interested, expecting our answer, once we were all seated at yet another, even longer, rectangle. Every head turned to us. We don't know, we said hesitatingly, smiling, that is why we've launched this committee. We felt a kind of shame saying this, like we were actually so inside the academic system, we were on the university level, everything a committee, everything another panel to breed more panels. Let's have a panel! writers say now, mimicking scholars, as if anything could be solved that way. Where? In a university classroom? A lecture hall? Worse: a conference center in the middle of some business downtown, where there is hardly any green space. The question of tone we suspected had to be solved in the outside, in the green space, in the open air. But we liked talking about tone with the people who were there; we were more interested in hearing what they had to say. Tone, we realized, had to be solved together; it was a question of the communal, of community. A grad student then offered that a professor once told them that tone was a window. This pleased us greatly. Yes! That's exactly what we have been thinking! we then said. Tone was a window that one looked out of. That made sense to us. This is what began this conversation between us, the idea of *windows*, of even more than that, *lighted windows*. We had just spoken about this, when it was our turn to talk, at the table that signified the panel. Not only an actual window in a room, for a speaker or character to look through, the inside to the outside world, although we are finding this narrative thread as well, with *The Rings of Saturn*'s narrator embodying the disembodied Gregor Samsa, with the grandmother polar bear perhaps standing looking into that same literary history, with our Helga Crane and how she hid from and saw the world. Train windows, hospital windows, windows of a flat, the non-windows of a cubicle or university room. Windows and nonwindows. The inside and outside. The narrative gaze. The overlap of the artificial and the natural. Somewhere in a text there resides tone. We still do not possess anything like a conclusive statement about these matters.

Light is a thing, we wrote once, but lighting is a relationship. There must be countless ways to light a room. Impossible to catalog all the varieties of relationship that can be afforded, arranged, and invited by the color and position of a lamp. We remember the masks and trickery of Arthur Conan Doyle's "The Adventure of the Yellow Face," the heat of sentiment, a cloying golden shade. The afterimage of that lonely window remains with us. We would like to investigate others, for we are not the Great Detective. We imagine ourselves a small detective, like Don Isidro Parodi, with his humble and mocking surname, who, in the stories by Honorio Bustos Domecq, solves mysteries from his cell in the Argentine National Penitentiary. We have an affection for Bustos Domecq, who has often served us as a model: this composite author created by Adolpho Bioy Casares and Jorge Luis Borges. In our letters we joke about this pair of collaborators, seeing them as our doubles, though each of us insists the other is Borges. They dreamed up Bustos Domecq while spending a week together at Bioy's father's estate. Each of them bequeathed him a family name: Bustos was a great-grandfather of Borges, Domecq a Bioy Casares ancestor. The impishness of their prank—played on the public, who thought for a time that Bustos Domecq was a real individual— percolates through the newspaper-style *crónicas* of the composite author, who describes, in ornate, inflated language, outrageous things like a tattooed suit coat or a restaurant that's totally dark. "In the long run," Borges wrote, "he ruled us with a rod of iron and to our amusement, and later to our dismay, he became utterly unlike ourselves, with his own whims, his own puns, and his own very elaborate style of writing." We take "to our dismay" as another joke; we imagine the two friends enjoying themselves hugely, following their creation as he strolled off to interview (in the words of their third co-conspirator, translator Norman Thomas di Giovanni) a "well-known but not yet famous novelist at his suburban retreat in Ezpeleta." The suburbs fill the writing of Bustos Domecq. They make its tone, a feeling we recognize, as if walking down the streets of our own hometown, the shabbiness of the featured novelist's dustcoat and bedroom slippers, his study like "the waiting room of a small-town dentist." A second-rate feel, the lighting a little dim. Pastel seascapes and china dogs. Bustos Domecq's writing exudes this provincial air, the portentous embroidered clauses of someone trying too hard to sound sophisticated, attempting to net, with his diction, a culture he can't quite reach. How dowdy we always feel in the city, behind the pace of life. At the outdoor luncheon that followed our conference panel, people were discussing matters of note, but one of us could not concentrate because the other's food had not arrived. What was this lengthy delay—everyone else was eating now—in the lunch of the one person at the table who was a nursing mother? Outraged, we picked at our potatoes and worked on suppressing our desire to feed the other by hand, a gesture we felt would not be understood. Tone is a window one looks out of and also a window one looks into, when one is a stranger outside on the street. We felt like the linguist traveler in Renee Gladman's *Event Factory*, navigating the mysterious city of Ravicka. In Ravicka, the air is yellow—the city is "large, yellow, and tender," the narrator tells us. The local language is complex, requiring gesture as well as sound, which opens a whole new field of potential miscommunication: for example, when asking to take a shower, if you make a scooping gesture with the right arm rather than the left, while mumbling and making eye contact, you will have delivered a deadly insult. The absurdity of this, how it captures the internal disarray of being a foreigner in the city, as the humor of Bustos Domecq distills the awkwardness of the provincial. Both texts, in their different ways, convey an outsider status through language, Bustos Domecq by overdoing it with circumlocution and hyperbole, Gladman's narrator by a spareness of expression that attests to the absent Ravickian gesture. At last the missing hamburger arrived. Now we could think again! How the body, even someone else's, can shift the quality of the light. In Ravicka, yellow sings out all the time, the linguist traveler explains, but the song you hear depends on your physical state and mood. Restored by the other's lunch, we joined in the conversation, describing the hotel where we had been lodged by the university, a self-described "art hotel" featuring a "Prohibition speakeasy-style bar." We recalled our arrival the previous night, how it felt like walking into a scene from an old film, the jazz band, the red piano, two old men singing that kind of music where they talk more than sing, joking with the tiny audience that was clearly composed of their friends. In the lobby, a young woman in a beret sat painting at an easel. When we mentioned this detail at the luncheon, one of the graduate students exclaimed, "That's tone!" The observation delighted us. Yes, tone is a hotel lobby artist who may or may not have been placed there by the management. Laughing, we felt again the elegant, jeweled hotel lighting, the sense we always have in the city of having gotten away with something, a conviction that we're not supposed to be here, but somehow we are, confirmed by the desk manager's shocked "Oh!" when we said we were checking in. We would like to clarify that this is not a pang of exclusion and sadness. It is a spark of glee. In Ravicka, the linguist is always on the outside, looking in, as if blocked by the transparent surface of a window, always frustrated and always entranced by the inner light, the yellow-green dawn turning gold, the "beautiful empty yellow."

"Architecture again," she writes. "It always comes to that. I can never get inside it; the singing structure eludes me." We realize that today, at the conference panel, we spoke about Marcel Proust in public for the first time. We rarely mention this writer even to friends, though we have been reading him for more than twenty years now. Why? Is it a variety of the impostor feeling, akin to the discomfiture of a Bustos Domecq gazing longingly toward Europe from what he considers the backwater of the Americas? Yes, probably, but more than that, we simply feel inadequate to the task of transmitting the embossed brilliancy of *In Search of Lost Time*, the slowly unfurling sentences that lavish their gilded riches not only on Parisian parlors and the costumes of duchesses but also—and this is what most delights us—on the little town of Combray. In our copy of *Swann's Way*, translated by C. K. Scott Moncrieff and Terence Kilmartin, Combray is "a trifle depressing, like its streets, whose houses, built of the blackened stone of the country, fronted with outside steps, capped with gables which projected long shadows downwards, were so dark that as soon as the sun began to go down one had to draw back the curtains in the sitting-room windows." The narrowness, the darkness of the sleepy town, the gleam of light in the windows. The snug, quiet rooms of the narrator's invalid aunt Léonie, smelling of linen, warm bread, and soot. Her *prie-dieu* and armchairs of stamped velvet, and the lemon-wood chest where she keeps her medical prescriptions and a statue of the Virgin. And the church of Combray, rapturously described over several pages, with its dark stone porch, its stained-glass windows sparkling through centuries of dust, and its steeple, the town's central landmark, visible from all over the place, even from the train, recording the passing seasons with subtle gradations of color. Architecture again. The singing structure eludes us. Something here of a vanished childhood, a lost state of mind, when it was possible to be happy with so little, happier in fact

than one has ever been since quitting the dreary, common-
place town for the wider world. We think of Proust in his
famous cork-lined room, connecting him to the suburban
writer interviewed by Bustos Domecq, who, restricting himself to writing within a "limited sector," has produced an opus
of 211 pages on the objects in the north-northeast corner of his
writing table. Is there a privacy to this writing that makes it
hard to talk about, a sense of enclosure, a hush? Nevertheless,
we did talk about Proust today, the scene of the death of the
writer Bergotte in *The Captive*, which, we remarked, immediately returned us to Nella Larsen's *Quicksand*, as Bergotte is
purportedly modeled on Anatole France, who wrote "The
Procurator of Judea," the story the ailing Helga Crane asks the
nurse to read aloud to her. Through the description of the writer's death in Proust's novel, this other body flickers, Helga
Crane's body worn out with childbearing, four children in four
years, her hair loose on the pillow, her filmy nightgown slip-
ping from her emaciated shoulder. We felt this doubling as we
spoke of Bergotte going out, despite the bed rest ordered by his
doctor, to an exhibition of Dutch painting, gazing at Vermeer's
View of Delft: blue figures, pink sand, and the "precious substance" of a patch of yellow wall. "That's how I ought to have
written," he thinks, mesmerized by the patch of color, like a
child trying to catch a yellow butterfly. How to write like that
luminous spot, that beautifully painted yellow that seems to
the ailing writer to weigh as much as his whole life? We are
still not sure. But we know that this is our research area: the
colored air breathed in with avidity by the dying man, as he

totters before the painting repeating dazedly to himself, "Little patch of yellow wall, with a sloping roof, little patch of yellow wall."

It was the previous summer that one of us first wrote to the other of lighted windows, after seeing the other perform in a virtual space, the twinning of lighted boxes. It is in these spaces of writing that we have usually been in communion, these boxes, rooms, windows. One of us wrote that we had previously thought of our longing for literature as composed of a series of lighted windows, that this longing was of the domestic variety, a desire for a series of interiors. The other responded, yes, a desire to find light in shadowed rooms. But perhaps, we write to each other, this longing for lighted windows is also an interest in spaces, of not only interior spaces, not only an I, but of imagining this space of and for others. I and You and We. Perhaps, we write to each other, this awareness of others, in their spaces, is something like ecological thinking, in that it approaches atmosphere. Thus began our informal, then formal investigations into tone, which may or may not be lighted windows. When we write to each other, we ask if the other has read Gerald Murnane's fiction *Border Districts*, which we were just looking through, stacked on the top of the couch, when we received the other's letter. How it happens that his report into memory begins with a digression on the stained-glass windows that he sees passing by his neighborhood Protestant church on his walks, on his way to the shops and the post office, which leads to an unfolding of memories and events in a rather circumscribed life, as Murnane has never left Australia, not to attend writer's festivals or to fly on an airplane. We open our copy of the book to a bookmark and see that Murnane is paraphrasing a quote by Franz Kafka, that a person might learn everything they need for salvation without leaving their room. Kafka was most likely speaking of the writing life, not salvation, and he was most likely speaking of men, or at least, that's how he viewed the writer's life, the life of the bachelor hermit, for certainly Kafka also didn't travel much. But keep to your room long enough, the Murnane narrator continues paraphrasing, and all could be revealed to you, which he takes to mean that he just needs to take a walk in his neighborhood, past doorways framed by colored panes, and he can move back into other architectural spaces of his memory. When thinking about this—about our longing for lighted windows, about Murnane's stained glass—we realize that we've never described to the other the church that we attended as a child, that the father of one of our committee members still attends, except when it was closed to him, over the past two years, that is one of his only frequented places out, except to the shops, and walking to the mailbox down the street. The stability of having a living parent who still lives in one's childhood home is also extremely discomfiting, as to revisit the place is to compete with and encroach on the instability and strangeness of memory. It seems urgent, to describe to the other, as best as we are able, because we are not the type to write about architecture well, to describe this church that still stands, where we spent so much of our time as a child, and the last time we truly remembered attending was our mother's funeral twenty years ago, although certainly that cannot be true, there must have been an Easter afterward when we attended mass, or the baptism of one of our nieces or nephews. We remember the feeling of kneeling on the homely wooden pews, the soft red indentations on our knees and elbows afterward, after speaking our venial sins in the darkened privacy of a wooden confessional box. We must have been around seven, kneeling by ourselves in the darkened back of the church, our fingers on the glass beads of our rosary, praying to be married someday to Christ, praying that we could be a nun someday. These were our first remembered encounters with beauty, that subject we have discoursed about so much with each over the years. The gold-lined prayer book we received at our First Communion, the white starched dress, the hand-sized book of the saints we would page through and memorize, the sparkle of our grandmother's rosaries she kept on the doily-lined top of her heavy wooden wardrobe. The sounds of the service as well, punctuating murmurs and organ chimes, so much of it relentlessly boring, yet somehow soothing in its repetitious, communal atmosphere. We would often play the piano for the choir, in our adolescence, as our piano teacher was the lead accompanist, and we remember the heavy red songbook we would lug up, stand next to, turn the pages, wearing church outfits like white silk button-down blouses and navy blue suede skirts, our hair pulled back in plastic tortoise-shell combs that bit into our scalps. Our entire childhood we were so dutiful, we followed after others, after instructions. We don't know if the other already knew this or could sense this. We are both from the Midwest, but we know that our Midwests are not the same. There is that moment in Hervé Guibert's *To the Friend Who*

Did Not Save My Life, after the funeral service, in which the Guibert narrator goes to the interment in the village where the Foucault character was born, but it's a different village than where the real-life philosopher is from. It is strange for the narrator to finally see the spaces of the estate of the provincial bourgeois family, with eighteenth-century paintings and gardens, his mother sitting stiffly and regally on a wingback chair, receiving visitors. There's a joy to this burial scene, something like the missing piece of his friend's narrative, kept so purposefully opaque, through folding screens and mirrors. To finally, only through his friend's funeral, see where he is from, imagine in some way his childhood.

As we read the above paragraphs, written the previous day, and during this cycle of our daughter's nap, as she lies across us, hands spread out, we realize we have never described to the other the layout of our childhood church. Ours was more like the Lutheran churches in the surrounding neighborhoods, known for their plainness. It was a circular church topped with a cross, located off the highway, with the connecting elementary school that we attended with our siblings. The steps to the altar were carpeted gray, and the altar itself was of white marble. The only elements of sparkle or color were the stained-glass windows, depicting, as was the way, the Stations of the Cross in mosaic. We are not sure if we ever really noticed the stained-glass windows. But as we sat in our family's pew, toward the front, we were aware of them, all around us. In the medieval ages the stained-glass windows provided illuminated narratives for the illiterate. The small pieces of glass were arranged to show patterns or pictures, assembled like a puzzle. They weren't there to reveal the world outside or to let the light in but to trap it, to trap the light and the color, to allow these scenes to glow.

Outside in our concrete city, there is the still the unbearable heat, the multiplying rats, the assemblages of trash on the streets. Yet the green in the summer is exquisite, even the campus lawns, even the green of the toxic algae at the lake at the park. The green glows. Is that tone? "I was outside; the relief I felt was tremendous." We forgot, reading *To After That (Toaf)*, Gladman's novel about following after a past novel, how much she was concerned with tone, about "the problem of the person in time and space." The various cities and apartment buildings where the speaker lives house the novel she is writing—she looks through windows at concrete trees. The places where the novella is written in its various drafts and notebooks and napkins, as well as where the novella is read by a community of friends, is actually the novella itself, from coffee shops to benches in large parks. Living spaces are also exterior spaces, walking through neighborhoods, both crowded and empty. "My challenge was to build, out of a series of empty spaces, a cohesive narrative long enough to be called a novella . . ." How disorienting to realize, for surely we've read this book many times before, that in the middle of the grid of this novella is a reflection on tone within Guibert's *To the Friend Who Did Not Save My Life*, a book we have spent much time residing within, thinking of how to describe it. Gladman the speaker realizes she had recorded a journal entry years earlier about reading the novel as well, the quality she describes as "flatness" or "ease," a narration almost without style, "the precise tone of the language." A feeling, she writes, of being close to the surface. Writing is moving through these surfaces. The sentences must echo the terrain. "Walking and thinking," she writes. The city and language together.

We propose that the lighted window is a zone of speculation. To be at the window is to invite a tone of fantasy: we are inside, imagining the shapes in the street, or outside, dreaming of the lamplit interior. We submit to our study the iridescence of invented language, like the phrase from Borges's "Tlön, Uqbar, Orbis Tertius," *hlör u fang axaxaxas mlö*, which means "the moon rose above the river," or, in the literal translation, "upward behind the onstreaming it mooned." The towers of Ravicka rise in our mind, cloaked in a golden haze. We see the people who speak in puffs of air, hiding in the cathedral. We hear the greeting *Gurantai*, accompanied by the appropriate gestures: the squeezing of lemons, the plié, and the tears. The fantasy landscape compels us because, by existing only in literature, it becomes an emblem of literature itself. The city is the book we long to enter. We are the linguist traveler who says, "The book held me; I leaned against it. I was waiting to be absorbed." This position of attention and expectancy is distilled for us in the tiny preposition *at*, which embraces both the intimacy and the mystery of a glowing pane of glass, the tone of the border, where dreams begin. *At* suggests imminent contact: an orientation or disorientation. Inside or outside, we are at the window.

Now, home again in our small town, we remember walking together in the city, among the huge trees of the park, talking eagerly, drinking in the brief togetherness. Our faces active, mobile, with their particular intelligence and radiance. How beautiful we were to us. We ate ice cream with the children. Afterward, there was a chilly hotel room, full of hard edges, so unlike the cozy bar downstairs. We wrote at the concrete table-top beneath the round flat light, copying the words of Glad-man's linguist into our notebook. "*Is* it possible to exist as two? To be doubly incapable of arrival?" It was appropriate, we thought, to be writing these words in a hotel room, a space used by others, its neatly made bed imprinted with the weight of strangers, its narrow window filled with the ghostly radiance of the city—an intimate space that nonetheless could not be called one's own. To write as the stranger, the person on the edge of events, at the surface of the glass. We thought again of Don Isidro in his jail cell, a place that, Bustos Domecq informs us, does not even have a window but into which the city flows through the visitors who arrive with mysteries to solve, with their various stories and quirks of speech. The writing of Bustos Domecq teems with styles, reveling equally in the French and Latin phrases of a pretentious *homme de lettres* and the slang of a character who spends his days at the movies. The Don Isidro stories are a hodgepodge of clichés, of used language, language that comes from elsewhere, from Europe, from Hollywood, from somewhere more sophisticated and desirable, a distinctly provincial language, we felt, as we wrote at our hotel table. These stories claim the world from the streets of Buenos Aires: Bustos Domecq dedicates tales to Alexander Pope, Franz Kafka, and the Prophet Muhammad, and packs them with foreign characters from Chinese missionaries to Russian princesses to expatriate Druses, yet this cosmopolitanism feels quaint, filtered through phrases like "*cela va sans dire*" and "on the lam," expressions that, Bustos Domecq implies, his characters have picked up to use in their own idiosyncratic ways, producing the feel of a backwater, like those far-flung neighborhoods where "they don't know a thing about urbanization, and all the streets end up in a labyrinth." Remote and crowded at once: a border tone. Today, at home in our suburban neighborhood, we read an essay by James Halford entitled "On the Edge of Conventional Maps: The Southern Mythologies of Argentina's Jorge Luis Borges and Australia's Gerald Murnane," which identifies both writers as voices from "the edge of modernity—the space between the plains and the city." They are drawn to the fringe, to raggedy regions where, Halford writes, the countryside "seems to survive" in urban spaces. We think of the narrator of Murnane's *Border Districts*, who writes in his own peculiarly provincial style, characterized in this case by a hesitant, diffident manner, laced with "perhaps" and "so-called" and "suppose," as if he is unsure of his right to his own language. Tuning his radio one evening, this narrator finds that words from elsewhere have penetrated his isolated existence, for "the voices from the sporting station, as it was called, were continually overridden by other, louder voices. I supposed," he goes on, "I was now so far from the capital city of my own state that my radio was receiving signals from across the border, perhaps even from the capital of the neighboring state." Keep to your room, and the world will be revealed to you, through the cacophony of your radio or some object that reaches you from a distant place, like the kaleidoscope the narrator receives from the wife of a friend, purchased in Roanoke, Virginia, about a hundred miles from where we are now writing these words. The kaleidoscope, a tube to which a glass marble is affixed, becomes one of the many windows that form subjects of meditation in *Border Districts*: surfaces that color and reveal, aiding the narrator's pursuit of mental images, or what we might call tone. Like our committee, the narrator imagines and hopes "that each of what I called my long-lost moods might be recollected and, perhaps, preserved if only I could look again at the precise shade or hue that had become connected with the mood—that had absorbed, as it were, or had been permeated with, one or more of the indefinable qualities that constitute what is called a mood or a state of feeling." In his borderland, at the permeable edge, he pursues his investigation of the tints that have seeped into his interior, of how language can produce atmosphere, like the word *Virginia*, which "denotes," he writes, "a small colored area in the widespread terrain of my mind." The narrator's image-Virginia is pale green with a ridge of dark blue in the background. "The pale green is intersected by dark-green stripes and studded by dark-green blotches." Despite the precision of the image, the narrator notes that "anyone observing the true appearance of a colored window is unable, for the time being, to observe through that window any more than a falsification of the so-called everyday world."

Perhaps this accounts for the difficulty of describing tone: how obvious it is and how hard to grasp. In Renee Gladman's *Prose Architectures*, the collection of drawings she worked on while writing the Ravicka books, we read, "Language has an energy that eludes verbal expression; this is a reflective energy, language dreaming of itself. I encounter these energies in the space between words, between sentences, in the crossing of passages, through the hum of thinking or imagining that shapes the language I'm reading or writing." Is tone the dream of language? "How were houses like paragraphs?" Gladman wonders, and we wonder, too: is it because, when looking through a window, you can't see the house you're in, and yet the house frames and arranges the experience of seeing, determining the position of the window and the angle of the light? How deeply verdant it is, our little town, as we write on the summer solstice, seated by the window in the unfading warmth, the sun absorbed and held in the piercing green of the young dogwood leaves outside, reflected from the darker, glossy rosebushes. We realize we have told the other almost nothing of the place where we live, perhaps mildly ashamed of its smallness, its unprepossessing name and history, or simply feeling that it's not worth talking about, that nothing happens here, it's neither a literary nor a commercial town. We have scarcely mentioned the long walks we have taken here, especially during the past two years, needing to get out of the house, to alter the scene around us, roaming the neighborhood in our straw hat, as we do now, despite the heat, suddenly wanting to enter the glow of the longest day. The light is thick, yolky. The streets feel abandoned, everyone staying inside to keep cool. Only cars pass us, though we hear a lawnmower in the distance, then the mournful wail of the train that rumbles through our town without stopping, scattering grain that will be picked up by the crows. Once we've turned off the main road, we can hear birds cheeping in the hedges. The cardinal's call: a series of falling notes, then a liquid chuckling. We have said nothing of the porches we love, with their swings and wind chimes, so deep they seem made for people to live there, out in the air, or the ones crowded with bicycles, furniture, buckets, plants, and tools, their sense of ongoing life, unfinished and exposed. Going downhill, toward the sun, it's as if we're walking directly into its molten heart. We pass the peeling house with boarded-up windows. The tiny house with lace curtains and a row of statues out front: the pumpkin, the twin spotted dogs, the painted roaring lion. A mossy birdhouse. A headless statue tipped over in the weeds. A stack of tires. The house whose front window is completely smothered with vines. We remember reading an essay by James Engelhardt and Jeremy Schraffenberger in which they claim that the vignette is an inherently ecological genre. The word *vignette* is French for *little vine*. In the eighteenth century, Engelhardt and Schraffenberger explain, it was used to describe a decorative pattern of twisting vines that framed a picture, creating the sense that the viewer was peering at the image through an ornate shrubbery. In the nineteenth century, with the advent of photography, the vines faded, and the vignette became a term for a photograph with a misty, dissolving edge. Citing the ecocritic Jonathan Skinner's statement that "Ecopoetics is border living, an irrepressible border practice," Engelhardt and Schraffenberger argue that the blurriness of the vignette calls attention to framing and edges and therefore to "ecotones." A vignette requires no storyline. It can surround whatever appears. An angel statue. A Confederate flag. Flies in the mulberry tree. A white wooden arch giving on a densely shaded green backyard that slopes down to the coolness of the creek. When the committee began our investigation, we did not know that we would write of these things. But if tone concerns ecology, then it is about making a space for relation, and it seems clear now that for us, in the end, our studies in atmosphere have been about making a space where certain things can be said.

ACKNOWLEDGMENTS

THE COMMITTEE to Investigate Atmosphere would like to thank the many committees whose work has inspired, undergirded, and infused this project. We took up our work in the spaces you created. Thank you Stefano Harney and Fred Moten for the single lighted classroom in a dark building; Lauren Berlant and Kathleen Stewart for the speculative playfulness of *The Hundreds*; the graduate seminar in Affect Theory at James Madison University, fall 2021, for the resonance of masked voices among mint-green walls; the yearlong lecture on The Animal at Sarah Lawrence College in fall 2022–spring 2023, for the moments of ensemble tone even through Zoom; the lunch outside at Le Monde near Columbia University in April 2022, with Hannah Kaplan, Hannah Gold, Julie Moon, Stacey Streshinsky, and Jenny Davidson; as well as Philip Leventhal and Caitlin Hurst, to whom we owe so much, along with everyone else at Columbia University Press responsible for making this a book. Thanks to Portia Munson, for the detail of your beautiful blue-tinted assemblage, and to PPOW Gallery. To the generosity of writers we deeply admire—Cristina Rivera Garza, Barbara Browning, and Jackie Wang. To our partners, Keith Miller and John Vincler, for reading and rereading with us. To Claire Fallon, for all of your expert help and attention. To Lisa Robertson, for the strange walks of the Office of Soft Architecture. To Bhanu Kapil, for the community feeling of *Ban en Banlieue*, as if writing could still feel like a blog and its comments sections. To everyone who stood in a room with us, at the coffee hours when we were guest writers, at adjunct cocktails where the full-timers had fled, and thought that talking about tone, thinking about tone, sounded exciting. As we took a walk together in Riverside Park, after that lunch at the end of April, exhausted from the day, we thought of Mark Fisher and Justin Barton's walk together in *On Vanishing Land*, and something of our project together, which was our thinking together, cohered. Perhaps, we thought, we could continue . . . ?

NOTES

ABBREVIATIONS OF PRINCIPAL EDITIONS USED

Bennett, Jane. *Vibrant Matter.* Durham, NC: Duke University Press, 2010. Referred to as *Vibrant.*

Berlant, Lauren. *Cruel Optimism.* Durham, NC: Duke University Press, 2011. Referred to as *Cruel.*

Fisher, Mark. *Capitalist Realism.* London: Zero, 2009. Referred to as *Capitalist.*

Geissler, Heike. *Seasonal Associate.* Trans. Katy Derbyshire. Los Angeles: Semiotext(e), 2018. Referred to as *Seasonal.*

Gladman, Renee. *Calamities.* Seattle, WA: Wave Books, 2016. Referred to as *Calamities.*

Harney, Stefano and Fred Moten. *The Undercommons: Fugitive Planning and Black Study.* Wivenhoe, NY: Minor Compositions, 2013. Referred to as *Undercommons.*

Kanai, Mieko. "Rabbits." In *Rabbits, Crabs, Etc.: Stories by Japanese Women.* Trans. Phyllis Birnbaum. Honolulu: University of Hawai'i Press, 1984. Referred to as *Rabbits.*

Kapil, Bhanu. *Humanimal: A Project for Future Children.* Berkeley, CA: Kelsey Street, 2009. Referred to as *Humanimal.*

Larsen, Nella. *Quicksand.* New York: Knopf, 1928. Referred to as *Quicksand.*

Ngai, Sianne. *Ugly Feelings*. Cambridge, MA: Harvard University Press, 2007. Referred to as *Ugly*.

Oyamada, Hiroko. *The Factory*. Trans. David Boyd. New York: New Directions, 2019. Referred to as *Factory*.

Sebald, W. G. *The Rings of Saturn*. Trans. Michael Hulse. New York: New Directions, 2016. Referred to as *Rings*.

Tawada, Yoko. *Memoirs of a Polar Bear*. Trans. Susan Bernofsky. New York: New Directions, 2016. Referred to as *Memoirs*.

I. FRONT MATTER, OR THE ZONE OF OUR MUTUAL SENSITIVITY

p. 3 ". . . the irritation of collaboration, as Fred Moten and Stefano Harney, together, have said": *Undercommons*, 117.

p. 4 "The strange thing about life . . .": Virginia Woolf, *Jacob's Room* (Cambridge: Cambridge University Press, 2020), 154.

II. FOG, OR A GRADUAL ACCUMULATION

p. 7 "Well into Helga's second year in Denmark . . .": *Quicksand*, 179.

p. 7 "gray . . . a gradual accumulation . . . fog": Morgan Aderton, class discussion, James Madison University, October 2021; used with permission.

p. 8 "fog has covered everything in gray absolute": Etel Adnan, *Sea and Fog* (New York: Nightboat, 2012), 15.

p. 8 "soft gloom": *Quicksand*, 1.

p. 8 "framing of light and shade": *Quicksand*, 2.

p. 9 ". . . much as Mark Fisher conceptualizes . . .": *Capitalist*.

p. 9 "organizing quality of feeling": *Ugly*, 174.

p. 10 "Black outdoors": Fred Moten and Saidiya Hartman, digitally recorded conversation, "The Black Outdoors: Humanities Futures After Property and Possession, Franklin Humanities Institute at Duke University, Durham, NC, September 2016, https://www.youtube.com/watch?v=t_tUZ6dybrc. First discovered in Aisha Sabatini Sloan, *Borealis* (Minneapolis, MN: Coffee House, 2021), 15.

p. 10 ". . . this pervasive *irritation* that Sianne Ngai writes of as the ugly feeling of *Quicksand*": Ngai, *Ugly*, 174–208.

p. 10 "'a faint hint of offishness' hovering about Helga": *Quicksand*, 74.

NOTES TO PAGES 10-14

p. 10 "... Helga's lack of responsiveness ... 'is likely to irritate the reader' ...": *Ugly*, 187.

p. 11 "... the right to opacity for Black artists ...": Édouard Glissant, *Poetics of Relation*, trans. Betsy Wing (Ann Arbor: University of Michigan Press, 1997), 189–94.

p. 11 "the freedom 'to *not* express'": *Ugly*, 15.

p. 11 "... as she 'passionately, tearfully, incoherently' speaks of her childhood ...": *Quicksand*, 86.

p. 11 "... as she weeps with 'great racking sobs' ...": *Quicksand*, 249.

p. 11 "like one insane, drowning every other clamor ...": *Quicksand*, 254.

p. 11 "... a form of praxis": here we are citing Sara Ahmed's concept of the "feminist killjoy." Sara Ahmed, *Living a Feminist Life* (Durham, NC: Duke University Press, 2017).

p. 12 "bare arms and neck growing out of the clinging red dress": *Quicksand*, 251.

p. 12 "covert omniscient narrator": Ngai, *Ugly*, 174.

p. 12 "psychological illegibility": Ngai, *Ugly*, 183.

p. 13 "skin like yellow satin": *Quicksand*, 3.

p. 13 "livid chalky white": Arthur Conan Doyle, "The Adventure of the Yellow Face," in *The Memoirs of Sherlock Holmes* (London: G. Newnes, Ltd. 1894), 141.

p. 13 "yellow livid face": Doyle, "The Adventure of the Yellow Face," 150.

p. 13 "with something set and rigid about it ...": Doyle, "The Adventure of the Yellow Face," 141.

p. 13 "coal black ... with all her white teeth flashing": Doyle, "The Adventure of the Yellow Face," 164.

p. 14 "is darker far than ever her father was": Doyle, "The Adventure of the Yellow Face," 166.

p. 14 "out of sympathy": Doyle, "The Adventure of the Yellow Face," 165.

p. 14 "little creature ... her mother's pet": Doyle, "The Adventure of the Yellow Face," 166.

p. 14 "of which I love to think": Doyle, "The Adventure of the Yellow Face," 168.

p. 14 "'Bless her little heart,' said he with a big hug ...": Charlotte Perkins Gilman, "The Yellow Wallpaper," *New England Magazine*, 1892, 27.

p. 14 "sickly sulphur tint": Gilman, "The Yellow Wallpaper," 11.

p 14 "sentimental 'mulatta' fiction": *Ugly*, 188.

p. 15 "Why, she wondered, didn't someone write *A Plea for Color?*": *Quicksand*, 39.

p. 15 "yellow . . . unctuous": *Quicksand*, 263.

p. 15 Paul Laurence Dunbar, "We Wear the Mask," in *The Complete Poems of Paul Laurence Dunbar* (New York: Dodd, Mead, 1922).

p. 15 "If I were forced to say a tone exists . . .": C. J. Bevins, course paper, James Madison University, October 2021; used with permission.

p. 16 ". . . giving tone more dimensionality than the New Critics . . .": *Ugly*, 28.

p. 16 "pale amber loveliness": *Quicksand*, 28–29.

p. 16 "luminous tones lurking in their dusky skins": *Quicksand*, 38.

p. 17 ". . . (Ngai observes here that her apartness is class inflected)": *Ugly*, 186.

p. 17 ". . . an observer . . . would have thought . . . would fasten": *Quicksand*, 2–3.

p. 18 "One enters a room and history follows . . .": Dionne Brand, *A Map to the Door of No Return* (Toronto: Vintage Canada, 2002), 25.

p. 18 ". . . what Christina Sharpe calls *the weather*": Christina Sharpe, "The Weather," in *In the Wake* (Durham, NC: Duke University Press, 2016), 102–34.

p. 18 "atmospheric density": Sharpe, "The Weather," 104.

p. 18 "She would sit quite still then . . .": Maria Judite de Carvalho, *Empty Wardrobes*, trans. Margaret Jull Costa (San Francisco: Two Lines, 2021), 5.

p. 19 "Modern Sub-Sub": *Ugly*, 176.

p. 19 "To write of diminishment in an extravagant way": referencing Kathryn Scanlan's interview with Crow Jonah Norlander, "Responding to Animals: Kathryn Scanlan Interviewed by Crow Jonah Norlander," *BOMB*, August 2022.

p. 20 "this bog into which she had strayed": *Quicksand*, 298.

p. 20 "she began to have her fifth child": *Quicksand*, 302.

III. THE WASTELAND, OR OUR OWN COLORLESS PATCH OF SKY

p. 24 *"almost total immobility"*: *Rings*, 3.

p. 24 *"colorless patch of sky"*: *Rings*, 4.

p. 24 *"a gray wasteland"*: *Rings*, 5.

p. 24 ". . . Sianne Ngai attempts to parse feeling from form:" *Ugly*, 38–88.

p. 25 "the Flaubert scholar described like Dürer's angel of melancholy": *Rings*, 9.

p. 25 "In August 1992 . . .": *Rings*, 3.

p. 26 "... Michael Hulse, with whom, we have read, Sebald had many battles": Carole Angier, *Speak, Silence* (New York: Bloomsbury, 2021).

p. 26 "Im August 1992, als die Hundstage ihrem Ende zugingen ...": W. G. Sebald, *Die Ringe des Saturn* (Frankfurt: Eichborn Verlag, 1995), 11.

p. 27 "circles of his spiralling prose," *Rings*, 19.

p. 27 "Borges ... on the artifice of dubbing movies": Jorge Luis Borges, "On Dubbing," in *Selected Nonfictions*, ed. Eliot Weinberger, trans. Esther Allen, Suzanne Jill Levine, and Eliot Weinberger (New York: Viking, 1999), 262.

p. 27 "His only means ...": *Rings*, 19.

p. 28 "Robert Macfarlane says that the American journey narrative ...": Robert Macfarlane as referenced by the director Grant Gee in *Patience (After Sebald)* (London: Illuminations, 2012).

p. 29 "... the Borges story that calls both mirrors and copulation sinister": Jorge Luis Borges, "Tlön, Uqbar, Orbis Tertius," in *Labyrinths*, trans. James E. Irby (New York: New Directions, 1962), 21.

p. 29 "If we view ourselves from a great height ...": *Rings*, 92.

p. 29 "We, the survivors ...": *Rings*, 125.

p. 29 "moral weight ...": Wayne Koestenbaum, *My 1980s & Other Essays* (New York: Farrar, Straus and Giroux, 2013), 90.

p. 29 "a certain sadness ...": Roberto Bolaño, *Last Evenings on Earth*, trans. Chris Andrews (New York: New Directions, 2006), 166.

p. 29 "Bolaño's supreme accomplishment ...": Koestenbaum, *My 1980s & Other Essays*, 89.

p. 30 "When the evening light streams in ...": *Rings*, 248.

p. 31 "... a grain of sand in the hem of Emma Bovary's dress could contain the whole of the Sahara": *Rings*, 8.

p. 31 "the circumcision knives of Joshua ...": *Rings*, 26.

p. 33 "tries to organize the fragments and part-objects ...": Eve Kosofsky Sedgwick, *Touching Feeling: Affect, Pedagogy, and Performativity* (Durham, NC: Duke University Press, 2003), 146.

p. 34 "This was Mark Fisher's critique of *The Rings of Saturn* ...": Mark Fisher, "Patience (After Sebald): Under the Sign of Saturn," *Sight and Sound*, April 2001.

p. 34 "global or organizing affect": *Ugly*, 28.

p. 34 "consciousness in its acquisitive mood": Susan Sontag, *On Photography* (New York: Farrar, Straus and Giroux, 1977) 3.

p. 34 "the white mist that rises from a body ...": *Rings*, 17.

p. 34 "through flowing white veils": *Rings*, 48.

p. 34 "half-fogged mirror": *Rings*, 70.

p. 34 "the white vapor that had carried his words ...": *Rings*, 181.

p. 35 "an effect achieved by Dürer, we read ...": Louis Marchesano, "Prints by Albrecht Dürer in the Getty Research Institute's Special Collections," *Getty Research Journal* 5 (2013): 173–82.

p. 35 "suggest[s] atmospheric perspective within ... vast vistas": Marchesano, "Prints by Albrecht Dürer," 177.

p. 35 "The air, between the eye and the object ...": Leonardo da Vinci, *A Treatise on Painting*, trans. John F. Rigaud (London: J. Taylor, High Holborn, 1802), 131.

p. 35 "thick air": da Vinci, *A Treatise on Painting*, 175.

p. 36 "mealy dust": *Rings*, 229.

p. 36 "pollen-fine dust that hung for a long time in the air": *Rings*, 229.

p. 36 "something nebulous, gauze-like ... a handful of dust is a desert": *Rings*, 80.

p. 36 "Mark Fisher's and Justin Barton's 2013 audio-essay": Mark Fisher and Justin Barton, *On Vanishing Land* (London: Hyperdub, 2019).

p. 37 "Brian Eno's composition": Brian Eno, *Ambient 4: On Land* (London, Editions EG, 1982).

p. 37 "I always thought that 'the voice' was meant to indicate ...": Fred Moten, interviewed by David S. Wallace, "Fred Moten's Radical Critique of the Present," *New Yorker*, April 2018.

p. 38 "an atmospheric commons": referencing Heather Davis's essay "Molecular Intimacy," *Avery Review: Climates, Architectures, and the Planetary Imaginary*, 2016, 209. Davis references Peter Sloterdijk's *Terror from the Air* (Los Angeles: Semiotext(e), 2009).

p. 38 "undercommons": referencing *Undercommons*.

p. 39 "[W]e are committed to the idea that study is what you do ...": *Undercommons*, 110.

p. 40 "Across what distances of time ...": *Rings*, 48.

IV. HOARD, OR AN UNAIRED ROOM

p. 42 "When is enough enough?": Dodie Bellamy, "Hoarding as *Écriture*," in *Bee Reaved* (Los Angeles, CA: Semiotext(e), 2021), 16.

p. 42 "I lift one to my mouth and suck ...": Bellamy, "Hoarding as *Écriture*," 23.

p. 42 "From now on ... you are me": *Seasonal*, 11.

p. 43 "stench of unwashed laundry . . .": *Seasonal*, 19.

p. 44 "No one's in the apartment . . .": *Seasonal*, 23.

p. 44 "matter of life and death": *Seasonal*, 11.

p. 44 "Work simply alters its own physical state . . .": *Seasonal*, 32.

p. 45 "contingent tableau": *Vibrant*, 5.

p. 45 ". . . like the branded knickknacks . . .": Dan Erickson, *Severance*, dir. Ben Stiller (Los Angeles: Red Hour Productions, 2022–).

p. 45 "You see a dust-coated stock museum; you like it": *Seasonal*, 43.

p. 46 "register of marvels": *Rings*, 273.

p. 46 "that already looks so lived in . . . nothing but a ragged piece of cloth . . .": *Seasonal*, 95.

p. 46 "thing-power": *Vibrant*, first use in the preface, xvi.

p. 46 "You're tempted to try it on for a moment . . . perhaps because . . .": *Seasonal*, 97.

p. 47 "one large men's black plastic work glove . . .": *Vibrant*, 4.

p. 47 "I stood enchanted . . .": Jane Bennett, "Powers of the Hoard: Further Notes on Material Agency," in *Animal, Vegetable, Mineral: Ethics and Objects*, ed. Jeffrey Jerome Cohen (Santa Barbara, CA: Punctum, 2012), 238.

p. 47 "It's because of all the things that are here . . .": *Seasonal*, 95.

p. 48 "We think about Lauren Berlant's concept of 'slow death'": *Cruel*, 95–120.

p. 48 "aquariums and luminous globes": *Seasonal*, 101.

p. 48 "Berlant . . . borrowing from David Harvey's positing . . .": *Cruel*, 95.

p. 49 "you suddenly understand the cocooning phenomenon . . .": *Seasonal*, 127.

p. 49 "Jane Bennett's essay . . .": Bennett, "Powers of the Hoard," 255.

p. 50 "You're one of them now, you see . . .": *Seasonal*, 61.

p. 50 "designed to serve as a stay against the frailties . . . aura of transcendence . . .": Susan Stewart, *On Longing* (Durham, NC: Duke University Press, 1992), 159.

p. 51 "We all use *du* around here . . .": Kevin Vennemann's translation of Geissler in "Seasonal Associate—Labor and Self in an Ocean of Time," afterword to *Seasonal*, 231.

p. 51 "entirely bereft of its secondary functionalities . . .": Vennemann, "Seasonal Associate," 231.

p. 51 "Now she's calling me . . .": *Factory*, 64.

p. 51 "muffled, manmade air": *Factory*, 65.

p. 51 "humanity-affirming formality": *Seasonal*, 232.

p. 52 "Fantasy is the means by which . . . What happens when those fantasies . . .": *Cruel*, 2.

p. 53 ". . . what Berlant calls an impasse . . .": See the following passage for Berlant's explanation of the term: "Usually an 'impasse' designates a time of dithering from which someone or some situation cannot move forward. In this book's adaptation, the impasse is a stretch of time in which one moves around with a sense that the world is at once intensely present and enigmatic, such that the activity of living demands both a wandering absorptive awareness and a hypervigilance that collects material that might help to clarify things, maintain one's sea legs, and coordinate the standard melodramatic crises with those processes that have not yet found their genre of event." *Cruel*, 4.

p. 54 ". . . Berlant's reading of Charles Johnson's story . . .": *Cruel*, 37–38.

p. 54 "in a jumble of people . . . spits out . . . You eat . . .": *Seasonal*, 55.

p. 54 "a nightmarish burden . . .": *Cruel*, 43.

p. 54 "why all the offal?": *Factory*, 38.

p. 54 "unnaturally straight": *Factory*, 28.

p. 55 "Raw blood will make you sick": *Factory*, 38.

p. 55 "I never found out how old Itsumi was": *Factory*, 39.

p. 55 "puts it in her mouth and eats it": *Cruel*, 37.

p. 55 "affective atmospheres are shared . . .": *Cruel*, 15.

p. 56 ". . . after Bakhtin on Rabelais . . .": Mikhail Bakhtin, *Rabelais and His World*, trans. Helene Iswolsky (Cambridge, MA: MIT Press, 1971).

p. 56 "Eating is *their* time . . .": *Cruel*, 135.

p. 56–59 "A bowl of miso soup . . . pink pickles on top": *Factory*, 11, 12, 25, 33, 37, 37–38, 38, 41, 51, 52–53, 54, 58, 62, 62, 63, 64, 67, 68, 88, 89, 106, 107.

p. 59 "In her own words . . .": David Boyd, "Hiroko Oyamada Wrote Her First Book, *The Factory*, in the Factory Where She Worked," *Literary Hub*, October 2020.

p. 59 "jump cuts . . . scenes that dissolve . . .": Parul Sehgal, "In 'The Factory,' a Mysterious Company Manufactures Fear," *New York Times*, December 2019.

p. 59 "virtual paper landscape . . . snow in the fields . . . a perfect kind of order": *Rings*, 8–9.

p. 60 "When my brother finishes . . .": *Factory*, 57.

p. 60 "squiggles and dots . . .": *Factory*, 54.

p. 60 "There in the dispatch hall . . .": *Seasonal*, 61.

p. 61 "I've put in your box . . . like a hidden treasure": *Seasonal*, 198.

p. 62 "desire lines . . . an example of perfect planning": *Seasonal*, 199, quoting Ryan Gander's *Loose Associations and Other Lectures* (Paris, France: one-star, 2007).

V. AVIARY, OR ANIMAL

p. 63 "Whenever we read this section . . .": Here we are indebted to Emily Jones's reading of *Rings*, "Animal Encounters and Ecological Anxiety in W. G. Sebald," in *Of Rocks, Mushrooms, and Animals: Material Ecocriticism in German-Speaking Cultures*, ed. Cecilia Novero (Dunedin, New Zealand: University of Otago, 2018).

p. 64 "the *are-bure-boke* quality of Japanese photobooks": Leo Rubinfien, "My Eyes Are Infamously Greedy," *New York Review of Books*, February 2021.

p. 64 Masahisa Fukase, *Ravens*, trans. Naoki Matsuyama (London: Mack, 2017).

p. 64 "Often—and my inmost self perhaps all the time . . .": Franz Kafka, *Letters to Felice*, trans. James Stern and Elisabeth Duckworth (New York: Schocken, 1967), 287.

p. 65 Thalia Field, *Personhood* (New York: New Directions, 2021).

p. 65 ". . . an abandoned parrot 'sanctuary' that is more chaotic prison environment . . .": For more reading on the alienation of parrot sanctuaries, Charles Siebert, "What Does a Parrot Know About PTSD?," *New York Times*, January 2016.

p. 65 "There is no subject: *there are only collective arrangements of utterance*": Gilles Deleuze and Félix Guattari, "What Is a Minor Literature?," trans. Robert Brinkley, *Mississippi Review* 11, no. 33 (Winter/Spring 1983): 18.

p. 65 "But is not everybody silent exactly in the same way?": Franz Kafka, *The Complete Stories*, trans. Willa and Edwin Muir, Tania and James Stern (New York: Schocken, 1971), 332.

p. 66 *Guideline on Odor in Ambient Air*, first general administrative regulation for the Federal Emission Control Act, instituted by the German government in August 2021.

p. 66 "an odor like that of an unseen bird . . .": *Rabbits*, 2.

p. 67 "The solo is an emanation of the ensemble": Fred Moten and Jarrett Earnest, "Fred Moten with Jarrett Earnest," *Brooklyn Rail*, November 2017.

p. 67 "strange animal smell . . . vile . . . made my stomach turn over": *Rabbits*, 4.

p. 67 "warm animal smell": *Rabbits*, 10.

p. 68 "startlingly pretty": *Rabbits*, 15.

p. 68 *"to dismantle the face"*: Gilles Deleuze, *Francis Bacon: The Logic of Sensation*, trans. Daniel W. Smith (Minneapolis: University of Minnesota Press, 2005), 19.

p. 68 "Now I am completely a rabbit": *Rabbits*, 15.

p. 68 "a world of pure intensities . . .": Gilles Deleuze and Félix Guattari, *Kafka: Toward a Minor Literature* (Minneapolis: University of Minnesota Press, 1986), 13.

p. 68 "Experience has taught me . . .": A. E. Housman, *The Name and Nature of Poetry* (Cambridge: Cambridge University Press, 1933), 47.

p. 69 "I looked up and saw a woman . . .": Boyd, "Hiroko Oyamada Wrote Her First Book, *The Factory*, in the Factory Where She Worked."

p. 70 "in that same spot, absolutely still": *Rabbits*, 16.

p. 70 "packed together like sheep": Ibrahim al-Koni, *The Bleeding of the Stone*, trans. May Jayyusi and Christopher Tingley (Northampton, MA: Interlink, 2013), 73.

p. 71 Ted Chiang, "The Great Silence," *Exhalation* (New York: Knopf, 2019).

p. 72 Donna Haraway, "Donna Haraway on the Humanimal," YouTube video uploaded by HUMAN, March 2013, https://www.youtube.com/watch?v =BUA_hRJU8J4.

p. 73 "zoopoetics,": Jacques Derrida, *The Animal That Therefore I Am*, trans. David Willis (New York, NY: Fordham University Press, 2008), 6.

p. 73 "pervading the interior,": *Rabbits*, 4.

p. 73 "like Donna Haraway's fingers linked together": This also calls to mind Donna Haraway's evocation of Eva Hayward's "fingery eyes" as a metaphor of the haptic-optic in *When Species Meet* (Minneapolis: University of Minnesota Press, 2008). Eva Hayward's "Fingery-Eyes: What I Learned from *Balanophyllia elegans*," in *The Encyclopedia of Human-Animal Relationships*, ed. Marc Bekoff (Westport, CT: Greenwood, 2007).

p. 73 "becoming . . . multiplicity . . . Thus packs, or multiplicity, continually transform . . .": Gilles Deleuze and Félix Guattari, *A Thousand Plateaus*, trans. Brian Massumi (Minneapolis: University of Minnesota Press, 1987), 249.

p. 74 "Her eyes were so focused on searching . . . more landscape than being": Clarice Lispector, *Complete Stories*, trans. Katrina Dodson (New York: New Directions, 2018), 227–28.

p. 75 "the view is always wrong . . . messengers and promises": John Berger, "Why Look at Animals?," in *About Looking* (New York: Pantheon, 1980), 2, 21.

p. 75 "we polish an animal mirror to look for ourselves": Donna Haraway, *Simians, Cyborgs, and Women: The Reinvention of Nature* (Abingdon: Routledge, 1991), 21.

p. 75 "an embodied, multiply-voiced utterance": In our reading of Humanimal, we are indebted to Sarah Dowling's essay "They Were Girls: Animality and Poetic Voice in Bhanu Kapil's 'Humanimal,'" *American Quarterly* 65, no. 3 (2013): 736.

p. 77 "the girl reached up, her arms criss-crossing rapidly": *Humanimal*, 15.

p. 77 "archipelago of Human Otherness": Sylvia Wynter, "Unsettling the Coloniality of Being/Power/Truth/Freedom: Towards the Human, After Man, Its Overrepresentation—An Argument," *CR: The New Centennial Review* 3, no. 3 (Fall 2003): 321.

p. 78 "The white European male face defines the apex . . .": Gerald L. Bruns, *On Ceasing to Be Human* (Redwood City, CA: Stanford University Press, 2010), 72.

p. 78 "vernix or matte": Bhanu Kapil, *Humanimal*, 21.

p. 78 "facial machine": Deleuze and Guattari, *A Thousand Plateaus*, 189.

p. 78 "the face is a politics": Deleuze and Guattari, *A Thousand Plateaus*, 181.

p. 78 "She destroyed the paper": *Humanimal*, 31.

p. 78 "Two faces blossom . . .": *Humanimal*, 26.

p. 79 "blue sky fiction": *Humanimal*, 13.

p. 79 "I saw gray . . .": *Factory*, 116.

p. 79 "Blue as blue . . .": *Humanimal*, 22.

p. 80 "I got back to the ship and lay down . . .": Herbert Mitgang, "Barry Lopez, a Writer Steeped in Arctic Values," *New York Times*, March 1986.

p. 82 "Polar bears don't make faces . . .": Melissa Eddy, quoting Doris Arndt in "Doris Arndt, Celebrated Animal Trainer, Is Dead at 88," *New York Times*, July 2018. Arndt originally said this to the Berlin newspaper *Taggespiegel* in 2007.

p. 82 "Time was a huge ice block . . .": *Memoirs*, 186.

p. 82 "The heard world was so commodious . . .": *Memoirs*, 181.

VI. GUEST LECTURE, OR REPORTS TO AN ACADEMY

p. 83 "Every conference is a circus": *Memoirs*, 7.

p. 84 "I felt this . . . like a stab . . .": *Memoirs*, 5.

p. 86 "I said '—' and made a certain gesture . . .": *Calamities*, 3.

p. 86 "The lecture hall itself may be nothing but a zoo": J. M. Coetzee, "Realism," in *Elizabeth Costello* (London: Penguin, 2004), 19.

p. 88 "The first thing I learned was . . .": Franz Kafka, "A Report to an Academy," in *The Complete Stories*, trans. Tania and James Stern (New York: Schocken, 1971).

p. 89 "We were trying to understand this problematic . . .": *Undercommons*, 117.

p. 90 "To get out somewhere . . .": Kafka, "A Report to an Academy," 285.

p. 92 "It's exhausting to be a guest . . .": Bhanu Kapil, *How to Wash a Heart* (Liverpool: Liverpool University Press, 2020), 4.

p. 93 "Where am I at this moment? . . .": *Memoirs*, 4.

p. 93 "No, I don't think so": Bhanu Kapil, *Ban en Banlieue* (New York: Nightboat, 2015), 9.

p. 94 "the distance between the narrator . . .": Matthew Salesses, citing Robert Boswell, in *Craft in the Real World* (New York: Catapult, 2021), 48.

p. 94 "country boy moves to the city . . . depends not only on how the author depicts . . .": Salesses, *Craft in the Real World*, 50.

p. 95 "All of Kafka's work is an exercise . . .": Roberto Calasso, *K.*, trans. Geoffrey Brock (New York: Knopf, 2005), 153.

p. 95 "This piping, which rises up . . .": Franz Kafka, "Josephine the Singer, Or the Mouse Folk," in *The Complete Stories*, trans. Tania and James Stern (New York: Schocken, 1971), 394.

p. 96 "At the beginning there's a wooden bridge . . .": Calasso, *K.*, 3.

VII. LIGHTED WINDOW, OR STUDIES IN ATMOSPHERE

p. 98 "I began the day thinking about . . .": *Calamities*, 66.

p. 101 "In the long run . . .": Jorge Luis Borges, "Autobiographical Notes," trans. Norman Thomas di Giovanni, *New Yorker*, September 1970.

p. 101 "well-known but not yet famous . . . waiting room of a small-town dentist": Jorge Luis Borges and Adolfo Bioy Casares, *Chronicles of Bustos Domecq*, trans. Norman Thomas di Giovanni (London: Allen Lane, 1967), 26.

p. 102 "large, yellow, and tender": Renee Gladman, *Event Factory* (St. Louis, MO: Dorothy, a publishing project, 2010), 11.

p. 103 "Architecture again. . . .": Gladman, *Event Factory*, 93.

p. 104 "a trifle depressing . . .": Marcel Proust, *Swann's Way*, trans. C. K. Scott Moncrieff and Terence Kilmartin (New York: Modern Library, 2003), 65.

p. 105 "limited sector": Borges and Bioy Casares, *Chronicles of Bustos Domecq*, 27.

p. 105 "precious substance . . . ought to have written": Marcel Proust, *In Search of Lost Time*, vol. 5: *The Captive and The Fugitive*, trans. C. K. Scott Moncrieff and Terence Kilmartin (New York: Modern Library, 2003), 244.

p. 106 "Little patch of yellow wall . . .": Proust, *In Search of Lost Time*, 5:245.

p. 106 Gerald Murnane, *Border Districts* (New York: Farrar, Straus and Giroux, 2017).

p. 108 Hervé Guibert, *To the Friend Who Did Not Save My Life*, trans. Linda Coverdale (South Pasadena, CA: Semiotext(e), 2020).

p. 110 "I was outside; the relief . . . the problem of the person . . .": Renee Gladman, *To After That (Toaf)* (Berkeley, CA: Atelos, 2008), 9.

p. 110 "My challenge was to build . . .": Gladman, *To After That (Toaf)*, 42.

p. 111 "Flatness . . . ease . . . the precise tone": Gladman, *To After That (Toaf)*, 49.

p. 111 "walking and thinking": Gladman, *To After That (Toaf)*, 51.

p. 111 "the moon rose . . . upward behind the onstreaming . . .": Jorge Luis Borges, "Tlön, Uqbar, Orbis Tertius," in *Labyrinths*, trans. Donald Yates and James Irby (New York: New Directions, 1962), 8.

p. 111 "The book held me . . .": Gladman, *Event Factory*, 121.

p. 112 "*Is* it possible to exist . . .": Gladman, *Event Factory*, 122.

p. 113 "*cela va sans dire*": Jorge Luis Borges and Adolfo Bioy Casares, *Six Problems for Don Isidro Parodi*, trans. Norman Thomas Di Giovanni (New York: Dutton, 2007), 101, 143.

p. 113 "on the lam": Borges and Bioy Casares, *Six Problems for Don Isidro Parodi*, 111.

p. 113 "they don't know a thing about urbanization . . .": Borges and Bioy Casares, *Six Problems for Don Isidro Parodi*, 30.

p. 113 "the edge of modernity": James Halford, "On the Edge of Conventional Maps: The Southern Mythologies of Argentina's Jorge Luis Borges and Australia's Gerald Murnane," *Journal of Iberian and Latin American Research* 27, no. 1 (2021): 59.

p. 113 "seems to survive": Halford, "On the Edge of Conventional Maps," 60.

p. 113 "the voices from the sporting station . . .": Murnane, *Border Districts*, 103.

p. 114 "that each of what I called my long-lost moods": Murnane, *Border Districts*, 55.

p. 114 "denotes a small colored area . . . anyone observing the true appearance . . .": Murnane, *Border Districts*, 51.

p. 115 "Language has an energy that eludes . . .": Renee Gladman, *Prose Architectures* (Seattle: Wave Books, 2016), x.

p. 116 James Engelhardt and Jeremy Schraffenberger, "Ecological Creative Writing," in *Creative Writing Practices for the Twenty-First Century*, ed. Alexandria Peary and Tom C. Hunley (Carbondale, IL: Southern Illinois University Press, 2015), 493.

p. 116 "Ecopoetics is border living . . .": Jonathan Skinner, "Small Fish Big Pond," *Angelaki: Journal of the Theoretical Humanities* 14, no. 2 (2009): 111.

Printed and bound by CPI Group (UK) Ltd, Croydon, CR0 4YY

22/01/2024

08225569-0002